TEN WORDS

An Interspiritual Guide to Becoming
Better People in a **Better World**

LAURYN AXELROD

THREE MOUNTAINS
PRESS

Three Mountains Press
1258 Betts Bridge Road
West Pawlet, VT 05775
www.threemountainscommunity.net

To purchase bulk copies, please contact the publisher.

First Edition

Ten Words: An Interspiritual Guide to Becoming Better People in a Better World

Paperback ISBN 979-8-9911059-0-3
Ebook ISBN 979-8-9911059-1-0

Library of Congress Cataloging-in-Publication application pending.

For my father, Jerry Axelrod, whose very being has been the teaching of how to be a better person in a better world all along.

For my mother, Vicki Fish Axelrod Barnhill Winters, who first taught me to love words and their meanings.

For my son, Joshua Montgomery, the inspiration for all my work. May you inherit a better world.

And for Patrick Lovitt/Lao Zhi Chang, whose life-changing teachings and skillful means of transmission continue to guide me.

ACKNOWLEDGMENTS

This book is the result of a lifetime of study, practice and exploration. In many ways, it is the capstone of all my years of spiritual seeking, wrestling with hard questions, and listening to the inner voice that urged me to find ways to help us become better people in a better world.

But no spiritual journey—or book—happens alone. We are guided and accompanied by so many people—some we know and some we never meet. My journey is no different. I stand in humble gratitude for the wise guidance, support, and friendship of so many, especially my teachers, those who have walked beside me on this journey, and those who will walk with me going forward.

Deep gratitude to members of Three Mountains Interspiritual Community, the first to explore Ten Words with me, and whose insights deepened this practice; my seminary cohort, teachers and deans; the readers and supporters of "Radical Spirituality," who encouraged me; my editor Lia Ottaviano and designer Steve Kuhn; and Rod Wilson, who patiently listened to me ramble and sermonize over tea or late at night as this book took shape.

This book wouldn't exist without you.

I bow.

Contents

Introduction

Each one of us must make his own true way,
and when we do, that way will express the universal way.
SHUNRYU SUZUKI

The young woman in front of me was in tears. Sitting on the edge of her chair, she twisted the hem of her dress anxiously as she spoke.

"The world is such a mess," she cried. "I just don't understand why we just can't get it right. What can we do—what can I do—to make it better?"

She is not alone. Many of us feel this way. I, too, have had many teary days and sleepless nights wondering how we got ourselves into this situation and what we can possibly do to get ourselves out of it. As an ordained Interfaith/Interspiritual minister, chaplain and spiritual counselor, I daily encounter people of all ages who are desperately asking these same questions…and coming up short.

It's not hard to feel overwhelmed today. We are surrounded with political upheavals, war, poverty, oppression, disease, inequality, injustice, and environmental destruction. And that's just what we see or experience in the external world. Our inner worlds are equally as pain-ful: many of us suffer from depression, anxiety, fear, rage, despair, and grief. We are confused; we seek answers. How can we heal ourselves and the world around us? How can we be better people in a better world?

None of this is new. From time immemorial, people have struggled to be better people in a better world and looked for guidance. Some looked to religion, mythology, divination, or philosophy, and more recently to psychology, science, politics, and economics. These days, the internet is filled with suggestion from all corners, and then some.

Many of these give us partial answers at best or feel-good Band-aids at worst: we can meditate, we can protest, we can pray, do our yoga, change our light bulbs and our diet, or we can look to God or science to save us. While some of these are useful, most are singular solutions and don't get us to all the way to what we really seek—a world where everything and everyone truly thrives. What we really need is a complete, simple set of guidelines that combines the best of what we know to help us become better people in a better world, today. We need a map.

§

Where can we find that map? For thousands of years, the traditional spiritual paths have been the antidote to fear, suffering, and confu-sion in an uncertain world, and they are straightforward. Indigenous traditions have their beliefs and methods, Abrahamic faiths, theirs, and Eastern religions, theirs.

Each of these have time-tested practices, teachings, and teachers that, if followed faithfully, can indeed lead to living lives of happi-ness, peace, joy, and genuine spiritual insight and connection. After all, at their heart, all wisdom paths are asking those same Big Three

Questions: Who am I? What is going on here? And how am I supposed to live in relationship to that? It's just that the answers can vary.

At the same time, many of these paths have become institutionalized and exclusive. For some of us, a singular tradition feels limiting, stifling, or even traumatizing. Many have left the religions of their birth, never to return. Others have sought to combine them with less restrictive or more appealing traditions. As a result, we have largely become an interfaith, interreligious, multi-belonging world. We are Christians who practice yoga, Jews who sit in Zen meditation, Buddhists who participate in indigenous ceremony, Muslims who attend sound healings, and atheists who practice Forest Bathing. Yet, many of us still aren't finding what we are looking for. Why are we not finding it? What's missing?

In his 1999 book, *The Mystic Heart: Discovering Universal Spirituality in the World's Religions*, Brother Wayne Teasdale, a Christian/Hindu monk, coined the term "Interspiritual" to express an understanding of the common roots of all religion and spiritual knowledge, or what is sometimes called The Perennial Wisdom. For Brother Wayne, Interspirituality was what modern seekers truly sought: a spiritual path that recognized a mystical truth that transcended the boundaries of institutionalized religion and, at the same time, acknowledged our common spiritual heritage.

The great teachers and teachings of Judaism, Christianity, Islam, Hinduism, Buddhism, Jainism, Sikhism, Daoism, Confucianism, and the Indigenous traditions all offer remarkably similar guidelines and practices to help us navigate the pain and suffering we experience individually and collectively. Each, in their own ways, teaches us how to become better people—happier, healthier, kinder, more content, and peaceful—in a world that supports all beings to thrive.

Many of these teachings are as relevant today as they were when they were first taught thousands of years ago. It is why they have stood the test of time. Others are a bit outdated or not useful in the modern world. But underneath their diversity, there is a common truth, an interspirituality, that is echoed across all the wisdom and faith traditions; if we humans take care of ourselves, one another, and our world, following fundamental natural laws or principles, we will live in happiness, peace, and harmony. We will be better people in a better world. If we don't, well, you can see how well that works.

§

Ten Words is a version of that underlying truth. It's my way of trying to answer those niggling questions we've been asking for millennia, but for today's world. Distilled from the teachings and practices of all the world's great faith and wisdom traditions supported by what we have learned from modern psychology and science, each of the Ten Words describes a specific common aspiration, principle, or a foundational way of being and behaving *that is true across the board* and will help us become better people in a better world. They cover both our inner worlds and our outer actions, or who we can be and how we can be with others. Taken together, the Ten Words give us a complete, holistic, and practical map of the path we need to today.

In many ways, we already know these things; they are the ways we behave when we are at our best. We've been doing them for thousands of years...or trying to. I didn't make them up and they aren't new. Ten Words simply organizes and articulates them in a holistic, contemporary, and practical way that is applicable and understandable for people in today's changing world.

Importantly, the Ten Words are not The Ten Commandments or the Buddhist Eightfold Path or any other set of proscribed ethics: they aren't "thou shalts," or "thou shalt nots," nor do they define what is "right" or "wrong." They don't say you have to fast for days, never swat a mosquito, meditate for years, pray all day, or crawl on your knees repenting. In fact, there is nothing that you must do or not do. They are not hard and fast rules, but practices and questions to be lived into and explored individually. What do they mean to *you*? How can they help *you* become a better person in a better world?

Moreover, you do not have to be religious to find them useful. Though derived from sacred teachings, there is no doctrine, no dogma, nothing you must believe. All of that is up to you to explore and discover. They do not define the Divine, though they do suggest that there is something—within or without or both—that is fundamental, potentially transformative, and with which you can be in relationship, if you so choose.

You can call it God, Spirit, The Sacred, Ultimate Reality, Mystery, Dao, Buddha-mind, your Higher or True Self…or nothing. How you understand that is up to you. For that reason, Ten Words is applicable to any faith tradition you follow, or for those who are "spiritual, but not religious" or "Nones." Those who consider themselves humanists or atheists can also use Ten Words to live a more humane life that creates better people in a better world *sans* the sacred.

Lastly, Ten Words isn't psychology, medicine, science, politics, economics, or sociology, though it incorporates wisdom from these disciplines. This book doesn't promise to make you more successful, richer, more attractive, or more powerful. Ten Words doesn't guarantee to cure illness, end war, hunger, the environmental crisis, or the many other ills of our modern, industrial, socio-political world, though, if we all followed this practice, I believe it would help. Ten Words also doesn't promise you will reach Nirvana, Heaven, or Enlightenment, but depending upon your beliefs, it might get you closer.

However, if you sincerely explore these ten simple words and put their wisdom into practice, they can help you become a kinder, happier, healthier person in a world that feels more connected, joyful, easeful, and supportive. And, as all the traditions teach us, it is by changing ourselves that we change the world.

This book begins with by explaining how to use Ten Words as a complete system, practice, guide or a map of the path towards becoming better people in a better world. Each of the following chapters explores one of the Ten Words with a short description of why the word is important and how it has been expressed across the many faith, wisdom, and secular traditions. Each chapter then suggests some concepts to explore, reflection questions, and simple practices to help bring the word, it's meaning, and relevance alive for you. The final chapters explore how to make Ten Words part of your life for years to come.

Ten Words can be used by individuals alone, but the process works best when there is a group (or even just a pair) of friends who walk beside one another on the journey. Friends or a group offer support and accountability, and our companions also share knowledge and insights from which we learn and grow. So, grab a buddy or a group and explore together.

§

I certainly don't claim to be Moses at Sinai, nor am I a Buddha, prophet, or saint. I am just an ordinary person struggling to answer those questions for myself and share what I have learned with others. Since I first began using Ten Words to teach and counsel others, hundreds of people have already embarked on a journey to explore and express them in their own lives.

Today, more than ever, we need an inclusive, relevant, and practical map to guide us to becoming better people in a better world for all. I believe that Ten Words is that guide. I am certain that if we each spend time with these ten simple words, explore them and apply their practices into our daily lives, we will find ourselves happier, more connected, more peaceful, and more fulfilled, and we will work with others to create a world where all beings thrive. We will become better people in a better world.

May it be so.

> *Yesterday I was clever, so I wanted to change the*
> *world. Today I am wise, so I am changing myself.*
>
> **RUMI**

How to Use
Ten Words

The spiritual journey is individual, highly personal.
It can't be organized or regulated. It isn't true that everyone
should follow one path. Listen to your own truth.

RAM DASS

While it is true an authentic spiritual journey can't be organized or regulated, it is helpful to have a direction or a guide to the terrain you will be exploring on the path. Ten Words is just a guide, a map. It gives you a home base and points you in the direction you want to go.

Like a map of the wilderness, Ten Words is just a representation of the terrain, not the terrain itself. It simply outlines the trail, the points of interest, and landmark features but doesn't tell you exactly what you will—or should—experience while you're there.

Also, like any map, it doesn't give you the destination. You might use a map to reach the summit of the mountain, or you might use it to get to the river swimming hole. The destination is up to you. Ten Words doesn't define it. The point is to go on the journey with an open mind and heart, see where it takes you, and remain open to what you discover. Ten Words provides the questions, not the answers.

THE TEN WORDS

If you are following a map, there are waypoints that mark your journey. The Ten Words are those waypoints. Each word is a step along the path, a resting place, guidepost, or a viewpoint: a place to stop, observe, and explore. Each word names a specific spiritual principle, aspiration, foundational quality, behavior, or way of being and behaving common to all spiritual traditions (and many secular ones) that we hope to embed and embody in our lives to become better people in a better world.

The words are the common core of all spiritual paths. These are not proscribed ethics from any specific cultural or religious belief. They aren't "thou shalts," and we are not defining what is "right" or "wrong." These are not The Ten Commandments, The Eightfold Path, or any other set of moral instructions from a particular path. Rather, they are fundamental principles of being and behaving with ourselves, others, and in relationship to the Sacred that appear across the many faith and wisdom traditions. They might be considered the common themes of human spirituality.

The words are single, simple, and familiar, but they are deceptively deep. Each one has levels of meaning that only become apparent as you explore them. In practice, each of the Ten Words is a question to be lived into. We are exploring what each word means to us, how we experience it, and how we want to apply it.

You will also notice that they each begin with an A, a B, or a C. They are the foundations or building blocks for becoming better people in a better world, and living with joy, peace, and purpose. They are as follows:

1. Attention
2. Acceptance
3. Authenticity
4. Benevolence
5. Balance
6. Contemplation
7. Creativity
8. Collaboration
9. Celebration
10. Care

The first five words are the internal basics: principles or ways of *being* that we cultivate as the building blocks of becoming better people. The next five are the organic or natural ways those foundational ways of being *can* show up in the real world. They are ways of *behaving,* or external manifestations of internal processes. They are how we live in relationship to each other and what we call sacred, or how we make a better world.

This is an inner journey *and* an outer one, and they go back and forth, like a Mobius strip, until inside and outside are indistinguishable. As we change our minds, our behavior changes, and the world changes, and vice versa. It's all one system. Ultimately, that's the point of an integrated life. When we walk our talk and talk our walk, we are centered in integrity or unity—one of the highest spiritual goals both individually and collectively.

Bear in mind that though the words appear as distinct, singular points on paper, they are not linear, nor do they exist independently of each other, but like a loop trail, they are holistically connected. As you go through them, you will see how they organically flow into each other. Over time, they become not singular steps or fixed points but evolving processes of continual inquiry that relate to and build on each other. As we explore and grow, they deepen, and the relationships between them become richer. They become one continuous path.

Ultimately, the focus of our journey—and the purpose of Ten Words—is to help us formulate and live our own authentic, integrated spiritual understanding and practice. Ten Words leads us to our own "why" and practical "how" of becoming better people in a better world, not a path dictated by external dogma but one that is authentic and useful to each of us. Most importantly, as we change, the world changes.

QUESTIONS, NOT ANSWERS

Everyone determines their own understanding and the specific ways each of the Ten Words appears in practice for themselves or the way they walk the path. There are no right answers, no one way to walk them, no fixed outcome; we grow into them and through them, and the intention and exploration each person brings to the process is the point.

Our beliefs, understandings, and behaviors will shift and change as we explore. We will grow. That's what we want. For that reason, we must approach our journey—and each of the Ten Words—with curiosity. It's an adventure. If we start a journey already thinking we know what it all means and what will happen, there's no point in going forward. If we do proceed, we will end up only knowing what we already knew. Instead, if we start with curiosity, an open mind, and a willingness to be surprised by what we find, we will be transformed.

We must start this journey from a place of not-knowing. As Zen teacher Shunryu Suzuki says, "'I don't know' is the First Principle." We must release any preconceived notions of what we think something is or means, what we think will happen, or what we think should happen. We must let go of any conditioned beliefs and get curious. We dig deeper, searching for what we might find below the surface. We ask: What does it really mean for me? What is my direct experience of it? What follows is an experiential, direct knowingness, which all the mystics discovered. That can start only from a place of not knowing.

That said, you can and should read and listen to what those who have come before say about the terrain we travel. We have had—and still have—some very wise teachers. Their words and experience provide inspiration and a jumping-off point. There are many resources, from spiritual texts, teachings, and teachers in all traditions to contemporary secular, scientific, and artistic works. Find the ones that work for you, explore widely, and push your boundaries. Don't limit yourself to what you already know. Guidance can be found in unexpected places.

Think about what you read or hear and try it out, but don't rely on what others have written or said to determine or define your experience. You must go on the journey yourself to truly understand it. Remember that the most important part of this journey is *your* experience. This is an inner journey as much as an outer one, a lived experience, not just an intellectual idea.

SET YOUR INTENTION

To begin, set your intention, your North: How do you hope to proceed on this journey? What is the direction you are going? What purpose guides you? Your intention at the outset orients you for the journey. It is like saying, "I intend to get to the summit of the mountain," or "I intend to walk slowly so I can appreciate all the wildflowers."

For example, my personal intention was "To explore the Ten Words with trust that it will guide me, to remain curious and open-minded, and let go of any expected outcome." Another traveler said, "My intention is to discover what I believe and how to put that into action." A third: "My intention is to become a kinder, more compassionate person and to have a closer relationship to Spirit."

As you begin your adventure, take the time to set your intention:

- What do you hope to experience?
- How do you plan to proceed?
- What qualities or behaviors do you plan to bring on this journey?

Be careful not to make your intention too specific or goal-oriented; both limit your experience. Instead, focus on a general attitude or direction that will guide you. Write your intention down in your journal so you can refer to it often. As on any journey, you might lose your sense of direction, and your intention can help you return to North.

FOLLOW THE TEN WORDS, STEP-BY-STEP

After setting your intention, begin your walk through each of the Ten Words, step-by-step. Think of each chapter as an introduction to the terrain of that area, an overview that points to things you might want to explore further. While each chapter explains the reason behind the word and offers concepts, quotes from various traditions, ideas to explore, reflection questions, and simple practices, the chapters don't give you all the information, nor do they capture what you might experience or discover for yourself. They are meant to be prompts that propel you to delve deeper.

Start with the first word, Attention. We always begin with Attention because without consciously turning our attention to the everyday details of our lives, our minds, hearts, the world, and the Divine, we won't get far up the path. Without Attention, we are walking blindfolded. It's the very first step from which everything else can be explored. Beginning with Attention is like making sure you have your eyes open and good boots on.

From there, move through the other nine words, one at a time. While it's tempting to pick one that calls to you and explore it, if you go step-by-step in order, there is a powerful way that each one builds on the next. You can—and should—repeatedly do this practice. It will differ each time but go in order the first time. Then, you can go out of sequence if and as you feel called. You can also return to a word whenever you want to explore further.

If possible, for your first journey with Ten Words, commit to taking a month for each word to explore and experience. It is possible to go through the words in a shorter time, and some people explore one a week for ten weeks. However, a month gives busy people a concentrated but ample period to truly explore while also allowing the word to work on you in a contemplative way. An interesting thing happens when you allow the time for the ideas to percolate; effortlessly, you move beyond the surface "knowing" of what you think each word means and begin to see things for what they really are. It becomes true inquiry.

Consider each word your theme for the week or month. If you do, you will notice how it starts to show up in all kinds of ways. It's like what happens when you walk in the forest and notice heart-shaped rocks or blue flowers. Soon, it seems you are surrounded by them! It's because you have tuned your eyes to find them. The same is true for the Ten Words. If you keep the word in front of you daily, you will begin to see it reflected in your life and environment, and your experience and understanding will deepen.

No matter how long you choose to spend on each word, read each chapter carefully and contemplatively, as many times as necessary. Allow it to prompt you. Spend time investigating the reflection questions for yourself. Try a few of the suggested practices. Journal. Read from other suggested teachings and traditions that might apply. Since the words are really questions to which we don't have the answers, think like an explorer in a strange land and investigate the unknown territory you are in.

Even if you don't use the Reflection Questions or the Suggested Practices in each chapter, there is a powerful way that Ten Words works on you. Some people write each word on a piece of paper stuck to their bathroom mirror or computer screen and find that it mysteriously, effortlessly seeps into their lives. However, if you do explore the questions and practices, your journey will deepen, and your experience will be that much richer.

KEEP TRACK

Throughout your journey, set aside specific times to read, reflect, practice different techniques, journal, or record your insights and experience in other ways. It is important to make regular time in your schedule for this. Maybe it's a few minutes each morning or evening or one day a week. Whatever you choose, make it something you can commit to and sincerely show up for it. One of the things we know about walking the spiritual path is that if you don't put the effort in, there will be no progress. So, set a time for your practice that works for you and commit to it. My teacher used to tell his students, "It doesn't matter what you do, just do it sincerely."

It is also very important that you keep a record of your journey. Taking a few moments each day to write down your thoughts, insights, and experiences will help you progress and remind you of everything you have discovered on the way. Think of your journal as your trail notes, describing your journey and what you want to remember later.

If you are working with a group, set regular times to meet to share, learn, celebrate, and practice, whether in person or virtually. At least once a month is a minimum. You might choose to meet weekly or bi-weekly to share, check in, or focus on different aspects of the words.

IN YOUR OWN WORDS

At the end of your exploration of the Ten Words, you are invited to put your learning into your own words by creating your own personal map, or your vows, oaths, commitments, practices, or code. Your personal map is based on your exploration of the Ten Words but specific to you, your life, and your understanding. Its purpose is to give you concrete actions to help you stay focused as you continue to become a better person in a better world. Chapter 11, in Part 2 of the book, gives detailed suggestions and instructions for how to do this.

LIVE THE TEN WORDS

Then, of course, keep going. The journey doesn't end there. It's just the beginning. You can go back through the Ten Words endlessly, and every time, you will experience something new and different. To quote the great Persian Sufi poet and mystic Rumi, "As you start to walk on the way, the way appears." This is a lifelong path. Let the Ten Words and their meanings guide you to becoming a better person in a better world, and finding peace, joy, and purpose in the process.

On Spiritual Terms
and Definitions

We call the Divine by so many different names: God, Adonai, YHWH, Elohim, Jehovah, Allah, Lord, Brahman, The Great Spirit, Buddha-mind, Mystery, Source, Infinite, Light, Love, Eternal, Beloved, The Sacred, The Ineffable, Ultimate Reality, Higher Power, True Self, The One, The Dao, Existence, and many, many, many others. Hebrew tradition says there are 72 names for God, Muslim tradition offers 99, and the Vedas say there are 3,306 or more.

In this book, you will see many different names used depending on the tradition. Try to approach each respectfully, recognizing it is only one of the many names people use. Though this book does not define the Divine or offer a specific name, when using Ten Words language, we often use "the Divine" or "the Sacred" as a generic.

PART 1

TEN WORDS

The spiritual life does not remove us from
the world but leads us deeper into it.
HENRI J.M. NOUWEN

1

Attention

To pay attention, this is our endless and proper work.
MARY OLIVER

The first of the Ten Words is Attention because *everything* follows from the placement and quality of our attention. Everything. You cannot see where you are going if your eyes aren't open. If your eyes aren't open, you will most certainly end up lost. Therefore, Attention is the first step and the foundation of everything we do on this path, and every spiritual practice is—in one way or another—about cultivating our ability to pay attention. One could say learning to pay attention is like learning how to walk. It's that basic.

Whether we know it or not, we are already on a spiritual journey just by being alive. Life itself is the path. The purpose of Attention, then, is to be present for life, to notice the path we are already on, to look around and see clearly where we are, what's around us, what we are thinking and feeling, and what's happening, so we can make real choices about where we want to go. It means to be present with what is happening in our lives. Without Attention, our lives slip by without noticing, and we miss the whole point of being alive...or on a spiritual journey…and we will have a much harder time becoming better people in a better world.

WHY IS ATTENTION IMPORTANT?

*When we mindfully pay attention to our present
experiences, we start to see God's hand in everything.*
ANONYMOUS

In all spiritual traditions, Attention is one of the cornerstones of a spiritual life, and most spiritual practices are about learning to pay attention to the details of our daily lives, minds, hearts, bodies, the world, and the Divine; we want to become fully conscious of reality and connected to it.

For Buddhists, Daoists, and Vedantic Hindus, Attention is the very essence of spiritual life. All practices and teachings are focused on learning to pay attention and to see with clarity and equanimity. Its importance is illustrated by this Zen story:

A monk once asked his teacher, "What is the fundamental teaching in Buddhism?"

The Master replied, "Attention."

The student, dissatisfied with the answer, said, "I wasn't asking about attention but for the essential teaching in Buddhism."

The Master replied, "Attention, Attention, Attention."

Learning to pay attention to the contents of our minds and lives allows us to be present to our lives instead of absent from them. It allows us to see things for what they are, not what we think, and respond from that understanding.

In modern spirituality, we often refer to Attention as Mindfulness. Mindfulness teacher Jon Kabat-Zinn explains it this way:

> Mindfulness means moment-to-moment, non-judgmental awareness. It is cultivated by refining our capacity to pay attention, intentionally, in the present moment, and then sustaining that attention over time as best we can. In the process, we become more in touch with our life as it is unfolding.

In addition to paying attention to what happens in our daily lives, our minds, and our hearts, every wisdom tradition emphasizes the importance of turning our attention toward the Divine, or the Ultimate Reality. The *Shema*, the most important prayer in Judaism, begins with the word *Shema*, or "Listen!" In other words, pay attention! In the Bible, there are numerous instances of Jesus telling his followers to pay attention to the ways of the Lord: "If you have eyes to see, ears to hear." In the Qur'an, the ways we are shown to attend to Allah are infinite, and the faithful are instructed to pay attention to the creations of Allah, i.e., the details of life and the world around them. In other words, by paying attention to our daily lives, we also pay attention to the Divine.

It isn't only spiritual teachers who say attention is important. Psychologists, neuroscientists, and biologists all concur that paying attention and focusing the mind have positive effects on our bodies, our minds, our behavior, and our relationships. Paying attention eases anxiety, depression, stress, addiction, aggression, physical illness, and pain and increases joy, happiness, and creativity. In some ways, science is just catching up to what the mystics always knew: Attention is the only way we truly live in connection with ourselves, others, the Divine, and the world around us. It's the basis for becoming better people in a better world.

HOW TO BRING ATTENTION INTO YOUR LIFE

Be Here Now
RAM DASS

Modern spirituality focuses on Attention or Mindfulness as the means of "living in the moment." Vietnamese Zen Buddhist monk and teacher Thich Nhat Hanh said, "The present moment is filled with joy and happiness. If you are attentive, you will see it." In other words, if we bring our awareness fully to each moment, we may discover the beauty and joy inherent in it.

We call it "being present," and "presence" is the quality that comes from it. The more we practice paying attention, the more attentive and present we become, and the fuller and more meaningful our lives are.

WHERE IS YOUR ATTENTION?

Before putting our attention anywhere, we must become aware of where our attention is. Our modern lives are filled with distractions. For those of us seeking a spiritual life, the clamor for attention can be challenging. Cell phones, TV, the internet, the news, the demands of others, endless urgent activities…it's no wonder we struggle.

It's not just external distractions. We tend to pay more attention to the rambling chatter of our minds than what is happening in front of us. Most of our attention is spent in the past, ruminating on what happened, or in the future, fantasizing about what might happen. We are rarely in the right here, right now.

Put simply, we aren't used to giving our full, open attention to each moment. We might be walking the dog while simultaneously talking on the phone, thinking about our day ahead, or replaying a conversation from last night in our minds. Sometimes, we think if we give our attention fully to one thing, we will miss something else. Maybe. But think about everything we gain when we give our attention to what is in front of us now. Zen teacher John Daido Loori says it succinctly: "If you miss the moment, you miss your life."

Try this: Sit comfortably and still. Close your eyes and pay attention to your thoughts for a few minutes. Don't judge them, just observe them. You will see exactly where your attention is: past conversations, future plans, the pain in your leg, the leak in the car, what you will eat for dinner, the to-do list that never ends. In other words, most of us discover our attention is all over the place. In fact, it is almost everywhere but here. This is our baseline; it's normal. But how do we get it here, now?

BE WHERE YOUR HANDS ARE

The first step in paying attention is to set the *intention* to pay attention. In Daoism, it is said that "Attention follows Intention." Attention is energy, and it is directed by our intent. In Hebrew, the word is *Kavannah*, which refers to the intention we must have when we pray; prayer without intention is ineffective; it's just recitation. The Arabic word for intention, as used in Islam, is *Niyyah*, and it is considered the prerequisite for any fruitful action. In other words, we must *intend* to *attend*. In fact, intention, or willingness, is the prerequisite for becoming better people in a better world.

The place we start with Attention is very simple (but simple doesn't mean easy). We *intend* to pay attention to what is present in the moment, moment by moment. Whether we are doing the dishes, walking the dog, skiing down a mountain, practicing yoga, or baking a cake, our task is to be as fully present to that moment as possible.

One way of thinking of it is to "Be where your hands are." In other words, we simply try to keep our attention on what is happening right here, right now, where our body is. Don't drift off elsewhere. Observe where you are without judging it, simply noticing. What do you see, hear, feel, or experience right here, right now? When we are not present, we observe that without judgment, too!

Mindfulness teachers stress that being present means letting go of what you think is happening, what you want to happen, or what you don't want to happen, and simply observing what *is* happening in all its details without judgment or trying to change it—just *this*. In fact, mindfulness, or paying attention, is really the art of being present to *what is*. In other words, what is real and right in front of our eyes. That's reality, and reality is where all the spiritual juice is. As Moses said when he beheld the Divine in the burning bush, "*Hineini*," or "Here I am, fully present to the here and now." We are always on Holy Ground.

Buddhist teacher Rick Fields says, "When we pay attention, whatever we are doing…is transformed and becomes a part of our spiritual path. We begin to notice details and textures that we never noticed before everyday life becomes clearer, sharper, and at the same time more spacious." As we said earlier, life is the spiritual path, we just have to pay attention to it!

HIT PAUSE

To train ourselves to pay attention, we must hit the pause button. Most of the time, our minds are on autopilot, running at top speed. Without consciously stopping ourselves to take a breath, even for a moment, inertia keeps us going. So, we must cultivate the capacity to stop, pause, breathe, and pay attention.

In monasteries around the world, there are bells or gongs that sound throughout the day to remind the monks and nuns to come back to attention. The sound of the *muezzin*, or the Muslim call to prayer five times a day, does a similar thing. Their purpose is to bring you to the present, to turn your attention to what matters.

But if you don't live in a monastery or follow Islam, you need something to bring you back to attention. Some people set a timer on their phone to remind themselves to pause for a minute and just come back to attention. Others choose an action they do every day, such as eating, drinking, cooking, brushing their teeth, or taking a shower, as a signal to stop, pause, and be present. One person I know stops to pay attention, to come back to noticing his breath, his body in the seat, and his hands on the wheel whenever he sees a "STOP" sign while driving.

The point is to practice bringing your attention back to the present moment. Just notice what is happening. Notice what's around you. Notice your body and where you are. Notice your thoughts. Don't judge, don't try to change anything, just notice. When you are paying full attention to one thing, you can't pay attention to anything else. It's impossible to hold two thoughts in your mind simultaneously. Focus on one thing at a time.

This is why breath is often used to train our attention. We must breathe, or we die. It's inescapable. We don't need any special tools or techniques. We can use our breath to focus our attention. Just breathe and stay focused on the breath going in and out. Notice that. Follow it. There is nothing more immediate, more present than the feeling of air going in and out of your body. Breath by breath, we come back to attention.

At any moment, we can stop and pay attention to what is happening in our thoughts, emotions, bodies, or environment. We can just hit "pause" and ask ourselves, "What's really going on here?" We can observe our inner experience and our outer one without judging, and from there, in that moment, we have a choice of how to move into the next moment. We live moment by moment. Each moment leads to the next, and the next, and the next. If we pay attention, we can decide how to respond, what steps to take, or what to do. That's how we become better people in a better world…moment by moment.

THE GIFT OF ATTENTION

Beyond the present moment, we must also explore where we put our attention in the rest of our lives and the world. Wherever we place our attention will affect us. In the age of distraction, placing our attention where it matters takes extra effort. What is important to you? What matters to you? To what will you attend? That goes for people, things, events, and activities. Again, Thich Nhat Hanh tells us, "The most precious gift we can offer anyone is our attention."

Conversely, where do we *not* want to put our attention? The Sufi poet Rumi said, "The art of knowing is knowing what to ignore." We only have so much attention to give, and in today's attention-grabbing world, everything and everyone wants some of it. Anything we give our attention will take over our thoughts and hearts. What is not worth wasting the precious gift of your attention on?

Moreover, how do we pay attention? Most of us are only paying partial attention to anything at any time. Half our attention is on what's happening elsewhere: The TV, the kids, what's outside, our own thoughts. Unless we are completely absorbed by what we are doing, what psychologist Mihály Csíkszentmihályi calls "Flow," we aren't giving it our full attention. Without full attention, we are simply scattered, like leaves in the wind, floating from one thing to the next without intention. Life just drifts by while we aren't watching.

It has been said that wholeheartedness is the willingness to give something your complete attention. When we give something or someone our generous, full attention, we develop an affectionate relationship with whatever we are attending to. That relationship often takes on the qualities of wonder and love.

Through that full and affectionate attention, there arises a sense of connection, of not being separate from that to which we are attending. The "I" concerned with all the monkey-mind details of our lives dissolves and is wholly absorbed into the object of our attention. Some call this becoming "self-less." I prefer to explain it as though the "self" expands to include everything else. Then, if you are paying attention, you will notice that there is no "I," no "other," just "we." Or, more precisely, there is just "this."

AWARENESS VS. ATTENTION

Attention and awareness are often used interchangeably. There is a subtle difference, however: giving our attention *to* something or listening *for* something versus attending to what arises with open, spacious awareness. Awareness is something that *is*, while attention is something we *do*. Attention *comes out* of awareness. We must have awareness before we can turn our attention to something. Awareness, or consciousness, is the base of our being.

Mindfulness meditation teachers often separate attention or awareness into three parts: calm, focused, or mindfulness. Calm Attention is often the first step: It's the pause button. Before we can turn our attention anywhere, we must simply get quiet, pause, breathe, and allow ourselves to rest. Calm Attention is just slowing down long enough to remember that you are here, now. It's a perfectly good place to start and is necessary for any other kind of Attention.

Next, there is Focused Attention. This is when we turn our attention to something specific: our bodies, our environment, our thoughts, our feelings, or something external like an object or candle. We release any preconceived notions, beliefs, or judgments about it and just notice what is happening. We are not trying to change it; rather, we are simply observing it.

In Focused Attention, we are concentrating our attention fully on the present moment in all its details. In Zen, this type of attention is called Beginner's Mind. We pay attention to what is happening as if we truly don't know—like a beginner—in each moment. This is also perfectly adequate; most of the time, you can stop there.

However, if you are fully present to the present without preconceived ideas, judgments, or thoughts, not trying to change anything, *and* not focusing on any object at all, simply resting open, receptive, and available without expectation to what arises, that is called Mindfulness, Zen's Empty Mind, or simply, awareness. Some refer to it simply as consciousness. This is another level of attention in which the quiet mind abides in that spacious awareness. It is said to be our true nature, our fundamental being, equivalent to the pure awareness or consciousness of the Divine itself from which everything arises. It's the penultimate form of Attention.

Rabbi Rami Shapiro calls that awareness "the I-ing that is God."

One way of thinking about it is to consider that God is in the space between our thoughts, in that abiding stillness. It is from that place that we can more easily direct or focus our attention. Plus, the longer we can be in that space, the more likely we will hear, see, experience, or be merged with our inner teacher, or whatever we call the Divine.

ATTENDING TO THE DIVINE

In all traditions, that is the ultimate experience of paying attention: to be merged with what we are giving our attention to, to be released from the illusion of a separate self, and to know ourselves as part and parcel of the Divine whole. In that experience, we discover the truth of who and what we really are. It has been said that "When you come to the end of yourself, you find the beginning of God."

At its root, living a spiritual life is about putting your attention to the many ways the Divine manifests in our lives...through the details of our lives. The poet of attention, Mary Oliver, writes, "I do not know how to pray/I do know how to pay attention." Paying attention is prayer, or communing with the Sacred that is present at all moments in everything, including us. If we aren't present to that present in the present, we may never know what the mystics of all traditions have taught us: God is everywhere. Just pay attention.

ATTENTION IS A FULL-TIME JOB

Ultimately, Attention is about cultivating a deeper awareness of ourselves, others, our connection to the world around us, and the workings of the Divine in our lives. As we explore Attention on our spiritual path, we discover that nothing escapes our attention. We must pay attention to:

- What we observe
- What we experience
- What we believe
- What we feel
- What we consume
- What we think about
- How we think about what we think about
- How we act
- How we speak
- How the Divine speaks or moves in us and the world around us
- And so much more

Every moment is another opportunity to pay attention. Christian monk and mystic Thomas Moore said, "Spirituality is seeded, germinates, sprouts and blossoms in the mundane. It is to be found and nurtured in the smallest of daily activities."

Episcopal Bishop Steven Charleston echoes this when he says, "I take out the garbage. I clean the toilets. I cook the meals. When do I have time to lead a spiritual life? The answer: when I take out the garbage, when I clean the toilets, when I cook the meals. ... Strive to be aware of the holy in the most mundane of things, and you will see it open up before you: the everyday is the abode of the eternal." Life is where the Divine lives.

Paying attention takes practice. It is a never-ending, full-time job, and we will always have times when we are not paying attention, but it's the very basis of becoming better people in a better world. It is also the means through which we explore the rest of the Ten Words, connect more deeply to ourselves, others, the world, and the Divine, and maybe even experience Enlightenment, which is just seeing what is with clarity. In some ways, Attention could be said to be the only real spiritual practice needed because everything requires it.

Everything changes; Everything is connected; Pay Attention.
JANE HIRSCHFIELD

REFLECTION QUESTIONS

1. What does Attention mean to me?

2. Why is Attention important for me?

3. Where is my attention?

4. What prevents me from paying attention?

5. What can I do to hit "pause?"

6. To what do I want to give my attention?

7. What do I not want to give my attention?

8. What is the quality of my attention?

9. What do I experience when I do pay attention?

10. What happens when I don't pay attention?

11. How do I pay attention to the Divine?

12. What do I do to cultivate my ability to pay attention?

SUGGESTED PRACTICES

1. Start with ten minutes of Mindfulness (Vipassana) Meditation each day. Just sit still in a comfortable and relaxed position and pay attention to your breath. Watch your thoughts without judging or following them. If you get distracted, come back to the breath. Build up to thirty minutes or longer.

2. Explore Buddhist or Daoist meditation practices that focus on sitting in empty awareness.

3. Use a Mindfulness Bell App (or some other regular activity) to remind you to pause and bring your attention to the present moment. Notice all the sensory details you can.

4. Take a walk. Keep your attention on your steps. Pay close attention to the sounds or what you see without judging or naming. Just observe.

5. Do a body scan. In a still, quiet position, bring your attention to each part of your body, noticing how it feels without judging it.

6. Eat mindfully. When you eat, eat slowly, and put your attention on the sensory experiences of eating.

7. Listen attentively to someone without interrupting. Focus not just on the words or what you are going to say next but on what's beyond the words.

Acceptance

Joy is being willing for things to be as they are.
CHARLOTTE JOKO BECK

Acceptance refers to the *unconditional* allowing of self, others, the Divine, and all situations and things to be exactly who and what they are in every moment, or accepting reality *as it is*, not how you think it is or want it to be. Acceptance isn't tolerance. Acceptance isn't approval. Acceptance isn't affirmation. It is simply the awareness and acknowledgment that something is what it is and *allowing* it to be that way. As Buddhist teacher Charlotte Joko Beck says, "There is one thing in life that you can always rely on: life being as it is."

Acceptance follows from the practice of Attention. If Attention is "It's just this," Acceptance is "It is what it is." When we pay attention to something and are fully present in the moment, letting go of our ideas, preferences, or judgments about it, we can accept things exactly as they are without wanting or needing them to change to be happy or content. It doesn't mean we have to like or approve of it, but it just is what it is, and we must accept that!

WHY IS ACCEPTANCE IMPORTANT?

Let reality be reality.

LAO ZHI CHANG

Every spiritual tradition teaches the importance of Acceptance to ease suffering, bring freedom or liberation, and bring us closer to the Divine. Both the Torah and The New Testament teach the value of Acceptance. Abraham, Moses, Job, and many other biblical characters and prophets are constantly taught to accept the will of God—or the way things are—whether they like it or not. Jesus also repeatedly taught his followers to accept God's will, even if they don't understand it: "Not my will, but thine." In Arabic, one of the most common sayings is "*In sha'allah*," or "If it be Allah's Will." In other words, things are what they are or will be what they will be. God will God.

Indigenous traditions also remind us that we are not in control and don't get to decide how things go. We can petition for assistance, but things are what they are because the Great Spirit has willed it so, and we need to accept that. By accepting it, we also see the Divine's hand in everything. In all these traditions, Acceptance leads to faith and trust. We have faith or trust that things are what they are and will be what they will be because the Divine is in charge, not us.

Hindu teachings also stress the importance of accepting the world exactly as it is, without our preconditioned beliefs or expectations so that we may observe and experience *Brahman*, or Ultimate Reality. For Daoists, accepting the natural beingness and movement of everything, unclouded by discriminations, distinctions, and names, brings us closer to understanding the formless Dao. In these traditions, the emphasis is on Acceptance as a means of achieving greater knowledge of and unity with the Divine Mystery at the root of everything.

The Buddha taught that the primary reason for suffering is non-acceptance. We suffer because we want things to be different than they are. He said that our desire for things to be different and our attachment to desire causes us to be dissatisfied and unhappy. We either want things to change or want them not to change, and that's the problem. If we can let go of our desires and our attachment to those desires and accept things as they are, especially their impermanence, we won't suffer—as much.

Radical Acceptance, a term in modern psychology (and the name of a book by psychologist and meditation teacher Tara Brach), says that while you may not be able to change the facts of a situation or a person or yourself, you can choose how you view it, and viewing it with acceptance and equanimity is the key to psychological health.

The benefits of Acceptance on the spiritual path are many: less pain and suffering, greater ease, better relationships, more ability to see the beauty, joy, and goodness in the world, gratitude, faith, trust, and ultimately, a deeper understanding and experience of the Divine.

HOW TO BRING ACCEPTANCE INTO YOUR LIFE

Surrender is the inner transition from
resistance to acceptance, from no to yes.
ECKHART TOLLE

One of the biggest obstacles to spiritual growth is refusing to see things—ourselves, other people, the world—as they are, without judging them to be good or bad, desirable or undesirable, or wanting them to be different than they are. But we all do it. All the time.

We are constantly judging. We judge ourselves, other people, and everything around us. We separate things into good or bad, what we like or don't like. We want things to be a certain way, we want people to be a certain way, we want to feel a certain way, we want life to be a certain way, and when it's not, we complain. Or, when it is the way we want it, but then it changes, we complain. We're never satisfied.

In the absence of Acceptance, we are constantly besieged by unhappiness. Sometimes, we blame others, ourselves, or God for things just not being the way we want them. We get righteous, indignant, and angry. We try to resist or change the flow of life. We want to control things so that we aren't unhappy. And how well does that work for us?

Every tradition tells us that fighting the way things are or trying to control the world is fruitless. There is a saying, "If you want to make God laugh, tell Him your plans." The fact is that we have very little control over other people or things. The only thing we can (try to) control is our reaction to them.

NOT TWO

Buddhism and Daoism both teach that as soon as you make a distinction between one thing and another, you create its opposite. You cannot have good if you don't also have bad. You cannot have right if you don't also have wrong. Duality is the issue. By the same token, when you hold opinions about things or people or make something a "problem," you cannot see the truth in its wholeness. Fundamentally, the trick to seeing and accepting things as they are is not to separate them into good/bad, like/dislike, valuable/worthless, not to say, "Not this," but "Yes, this too." Reality is not an "either/or" but a "both/and" or "neither/nor" proposition. Let go of the distinctions. It just is what it is.

If we stop trying to resist what is, control, or change things based on our desire to make the world the way we want it, we can see options when we only saw our way or the wrong way—another duality. When we learn to say "Yes" to how the world is, and not "Yes, but…" or "No," things flow. We may not like how it flows, but as my teacher, Lao Zhi Chang, said, "The Dao will Dao, no matter what you think about it." Our judgments—our "Yes, but…" and "No"—often stop us from accepting even that! We even think we know how the Divine should operate, and it should work how we want it to! That takes some *chutzpah*, but we all have it.

DON'T BELIEVE
EVERYTHING YOU THINK

Our judgments come from our beliefs and conditioning. Our beliefs are determined by our environment: our families, culture, religious beliefs, education, media, and our communities. From the moment we are born, we are conditioned to believe certain things, and many of them are so embedded we don't realize they are beliefs. We think they are facts. Like a goldfish swimming in a fishbowl, we are so used to it we don't even know we are in a bowl! But these conditioned beliefs form the basis of how we view ourselves, others, and the world around us, and they cloud our ability to see things for what they are.

The process of coming to Acceptance is through noticing, examining, and questioning our conditioned beliefs and judgments. We must pay attention to what we believe and the stories we hold about ourselves, others, and the world around us—even concepts of the Divine or spirituality—and challenge those beliefs to release them. In plain English, don't believe everything you think. Question it. That said, it's virtually impossible to ferret out every single one of our judgments and beliefs until they show up in practice. We must be mindful when they do and keep coming back to Acceptance.

If we can see without judging or distinction, then we will see ourselves, people, things, or situations just as they are in their complex fullness: perfection, just as it is. After all, when have you ever looked at a sunset and thought, "Not good enough. That could use a little more orange in the lower left?" When you observe a blooming wildflower missing a petal, do you judge it as not being beautiful enough? Can we see ourselves, others, and the world the same way we look at a sunset or a flower? Maybe the same way the Divine sees it, with absolute, unconditional acceptance.

ACCEPT YOURSELF

For many of us, this is one of the most challenging practices. We are constantly judging ourselves as not good enough or not worthy of love, "less than" compared to others, failing miserably in some way or simply imperfect in others, thinking we "should" be one thing, not another. We are on a never-ending, self-flagellating, denigrating war with ourselves, and to quell our discontent, we embark on harsh self-improvement campaigns to make ourselves good enough. Then we beat ourselves up for not being good enough at that, too!

Unfortunately, religions have contributed to this. While the fundamental mystical teachings of all religions say that we are perfect just as we are, some religions teach that we are inherently "bad" or "sinful" and can only be saved by accepting a certain faith, certain rituals, or the powers of an external deity. For many, this belief can be destructive. Even Buddhism, which has no judging, creator deity, can be misinterpreted to make us think that we are always failing because we still have desires and attachments, we can't quiet our minds, or we haven't achieved enlightenment. We are "bad" Buddhists.

It's not just theology that makes us think we are "bad," "wrong," or "broken." We live in a world where that concept is as prevalent as the air. Advertising, education, parents, and even the contemporary self-help and healing movements focus on our "brokenness" that needs fixing, convince us that our emotions are "wrong" and must be corrected, or tell us our needs or preferences are "bad" and must be changed. No wonder we have a hard time accepting ourselves.

There are also judgments and stories we have about ourselves that are deeply buried. In psychology, we talk about accepting our shadow selves, or the parts of us we have denied, pushed down, rejected, or refused a seat at the table because somehow, somewhere, we have decided (or were told) they are unacceptable or "bad." Our shadows are parts of us, too. If we don't accept them and give them a safe place in the whole of us, we can project them onto others, and they will wreak havoc on our lives.

The key to self-acceptance is the examination of the judgments, beliefs, and stories we have about ourselves and accepting the whole of ourselves just as we are in each moment. That means accepting what is "good" as well as what is "bad." As meditation teacher and psychologist Tara Brach says, "The way out of our cage begins with accepting absolutely everything about ourselves and our lives, by embracing with wakefulness and care our moment-to-moment experience."

That means we accept ourselves fully as we are in this moment, no matter what. If you are angry, accept it. If you are sad, accept it. If you are less than satisfied with yourself or comparing yourself to someone else, accept that gently. Just notice it. Notice where that feeling comes from and question its truth, but also notice that the feeling doesn't need to change in the moment. Try to see yourself through the eyes of the Divine, which, according to all traditions, sees and accepts you for who you are in your perfect wholeness.

Of course, accepting yourself doesn't mean you become complacent. Acceptance is not an excuse. We all have things we work on—which is really our spiritual path to becoming better people in a better world—but if we can't accept ourselves the way we are, we can't change. The difference is that we do it because we truly want to, not because of a belief that tells us we are broken, wrong, or bad and must change or are unworthy. Just as Zen teacher Shunryu Suzuki says, "You are perfect as you are, and there is always room for improvement."

As we come to accept ourselves wholly and unconditionally, we release shame, guilt, and anxiety, and we begin to find joy in our lives exactly as they are. Moreover, if we can accept our less-than-perfect selves *just as we are*, we will also be better able to accept others *just as they are* and the world *just as it is*.

ACCEPT OTHERS

Humans are hardwired to "other." We create a division between me and not-me, us and them, and judge others as different and not worthy. And yet, every tradition urges us to see others not as different than ourselves but as one and the same, not to judge others, but to accept others as imperfectly perfect humans, just like us.

The Torah, the Bible, and the Qur'an are filled with exhortations to accept others as God does: equally. "Accept one another, then, just as Christ accepted you, in order to bring praise to God," says the Bible (Romans 15:7). In the book of Leviticus in the Hebrew Bible, it is said, "…judge your neighbor fairly" (19:16-17), and in the Qu'ran, it is said that the only judge is Allah; we are not to judge others.

The Hindus, Buddhists, and Daoists likewise remind us to see everyone and everything in their unconditioned wholeness as manifestations of Brahman, Buddha-mind, or The Dao. Indigenous traditions all teach that we are inseparable from each other and, thus, must treat others with acceptance. Even 12-step programs teach, "Identify, don't compare."

Yet, we all have ways we judge others based on our beliefs and what we have been taught in our families, cultures, media, or religions. We judge our families, friends, and partners for not being the way we want them to be or for doing things we don't like. We try to change them, control them, or cast them aside. We have hidden biases that aren't conscious but still affect our ability to accept others as they are.

We must question our beliefs and biases and the stories we tell about others. We must see and accept others for who they are, even if they aren't like us. It's the only way we learn to get along with each other. In his Nobel Peace Prize acceptance speech, His Holiness, The 14th Dalai Lama said, "Accepting others' differences is the first step toward building a more inclusive and compassionate world."

What if we don't have a belief or bias and just don't like what someone says or does? Maybe our partner leaves the kitchen a mess, our children forget to call on our birthday, a friend betrays us, or our boss yells at us. Separating the person from the behavior is key to accepting others. We sometimes say or do things that are less than ideal; we all have bad days and make mistakes—even really awful, unfathomably destructive ones. None of us is perfect.

You don't have to like what people do but accepting it and learning to separate a person from the behavior says, "You are not what you do; you are more than that." This is seeing the Divine in each person, regardless of their actions. In doing so, we are looking at the other through God's eyes. *Namaste.* The Divine in me bows to the Divine in you.

Sufi teacher Richard Shelquist says it beautifully:

> It is often said that "all people are created equally," yet some are crippled, some are blind, some are deaf… so where is the "equality"? The equality is in the gifts of the heart. The physical world is full of differences and distinctions, yet there burns in every heart the same One Flame. Spiritual awakening is the process of realizing this One Flame, bringing it forth into the world in all its glory.

It is critical that we begin to examine our beliefs and biases about other people and be mindful if we are judging them and thus not accepting them unconditionally. When we do, we see they are so much more than we had limited them to be through our judgments or beliefs. They open like a flower, and we are often surprised by the beauty we see.

That said, acceptance of others doesn't mean we are giving a free pass for harmful behavior. But, if we could see them in their holiness and put ourselves in their shoes, with everything they have experienced or been taught, in whatever situation they are in, we might be able to understand that they were simply acting in the only way they could at the time. Understanding offers acceptance, which leads to compassion.

According to Sufi teacher Dr. Farid Mostamand, "A student once asked Rumi, What is hatred? He answered: Non-acceptance of the person as he is. If we accept a person unconditionally, it becomes love." Can you recall a time you felt totally, unconditionally accepted? What did that feel like? Can you recall a time you fell in love with someone or something? Did you not accept them in all their whole-ness? Maybe love is just that: Unconditional, total acceptance of the other exactly as they are.

ACCEPT REALITY

All traditions teach us to accept reality, or life as it is, whether by calling it God's Will, the play of *Lila*, the laws of nature, or the Dao. Whether we have fortune or misfortune, we are called to accept it equally. This is not always easy; after all, we like it when things are going our way. When that happens, we happily accept and even offer thanks. But, as soon as things don't go our way, we refuse to accept it and get angry. We must keep in mind what spiritual teacher Alan Cohen tells us: "Sometimes when things seem to be going wrong, they are going right for reasons you are yet to understand."

Some traditions claim that things not going our way is the Divine's way of teaching us equanimity, patience, faith, or trust in the Divine's greater plan. They say the world isn't how we want it, but we must trust that it's all in Divine Order, even if we don't understand or agree with it. In many traditions, we are taught to accept challenges not only as part of life but to do so with gratitude for what we can learn from them.

That's not easy when we lose our jobs, our country is ravaged by war or disaster, or we are hungry or ill. It's not easy when we do everything "right" but still encounter misfortunes or when innocent children suffer through no fault of their own. Bad things happen to good people, and that's hard to accept because we are taught—in reli-gion and by parents and society—that if we are good, good things will come to us. Unfortunately, that's not always true, and it's not fair. But it's reality.

This gets tricky when we consider the world at large. We might not like how our government works, or our economic system or our justice system. We might not like that some people have far more than others who endure poverty or oppression, but we must accept it. We are, after all, not in charge, and despite our deep wish otherwise, some things just aren't fair. It is said that the Dao is benevolent but impartial. Even the Bible teaches that God does not play favorites (despite what some traditions might have you believe).

That doesn't mean we have to agree with injustice, support oppression, or encourage what some call "Unnecessary Suffering." Still, we must recognize that we may have judgments or beliefs about how the world "should" be—ideas or ideals that may or may not be true or even possible and are preventing us from seeing the reality of things as they are. We are often outraged because the world isn't living up to our "shoulds." By the same token, we might overlook the "good" in the world because it isn't "good enough."

We can and should make efforts to change systems, structures, or situations that are unjust, harmful, and do not support the natural thriving of people and the planet in an effort to "complete the world," as the Kabbalists say, or to bring the Kingdom of Heaven to earth. But if we can't see these situations clearly for what they are—not our judgments, ideas, ideals, or beliefs about them—and accept that they are the way they are, how can we ever improve them?

In the words of Carl Jung, "We cannot change anything unless we accept it. Condemnation does not liberate; it oppresses." When we look at the world with Acceptance, there are more options for how things can be; it's not as black and white as we imagine. Moreover, if we do work to change things, we must learn to let go of the outcome. It isn't up to us. We must accept that.

ACCEPT CHANGE

One of our most profound challenges is that once we have things the way we like them, they don't stay that way forever. Accepting that things change is hard for us. There is change we like and change we resist. We lose people and things we love. Our company gets sold, our neighborhood changes, the weather gets cold and rainy or sunny and hot. We, too, change and die. Death, the only reality for everything, is the most profound example of impermanence.

Mystics from all faiths—and modern physics—teach that all things change. It's a fundamental law of the Universe. Some might call it the underlying principle of life. The Divine may be unchanging, but things arise and pass, are born and die, and every moment is lost to the next. It's always happening, everywhere, on all levels. Nothing is permanent.

Zen master Shunryu Suzuki writes, "To find perfect composure in the midst of change is to find nirvana." Working with and accepting impermanence is one of the hardest things to do but the most necessary. When we can accept that all things change, whether they change the way we want or not, we can more easily accept that we change, others change, and the world changes. More importantly, we can accept life, death, and the Divine on its own terms, not ours. Then, we are better positioned to move through life with equanimity and joy, accepting that things may not be what we want, but we can still be happy.

God grant me the serenity to accept the things
I cannot change, the courage to change the things
I can, and the wisdom to know the difference.
THE SERENITY PRAYER

REFLECTION QUESTIONS

1. What does Acceptance mean for me?

2. Why is Acceptance important to me?

3. What distinctions do I make?

4. What do I experience when I don't accept? When I do?

5. What prevents me from accepting myself? What would help me accept myself?

6. What prevents me from accepting others? What would help me accept others?

7. What prevents me from accepting the world as it is? What would help me accept the world as it is, good and bad?

8. Where am I trying to change others to conform to my beliefs or judgments?

9. Where do I try to control or change the way things are because of my ideas or judgments?

10. Where do I struggle with accepting change or impermanence? What would help me accept change?

SUGGESTED PRACTICES

1. Make lists. What judgments or ideas do you have about yourself that keep you from accepting yourself as you are? Others? The world? You'll be surprised how many you have. Don't judge yourself, but for each one, ask where you got that idea (if it is true) and if it would be easier to accept yourself, others, the world, or a situation if you let it go.

2. Attention to the present moment is the best way to practice Acceptance. It is very difficult to be fully present, without judgment or preconceived ideas, and not accept what you experience. Practice letting go of judgment for one day.

3. Practice saying "Yes" to everyone and everything. A full-hearted, unconditional "Yes!" to the wholeness of who or what they are. Catch yourself if it's a qualifying "Yes, but…" or you find yourself resisting with "No!" Just notice it and see if you can release it into "Yes!"

4. Many traditions emphasize the need to surrender our will to the will of the Divine. Practice letting the Divine take the wheel and releasing you from the need to control or change things. Just try repeating, "Not my will, but the will of the Divine," or "You take the wheel," "I surrender," or whatever phrase works for you.

5. Practice seeing and accepting the Divine hand in everything. If we can see it in a flower or a sunset, why not in a parking lot or even an earthquake?

3

Authenticity

The authentic self is the soul made visible.
SARAH BAN BREATHNACH

On the spiritual path to becoming better people in a better world, Authenticity is what spirituality looks like in practice. Authenticity means "real," "true," or "integrity." To be "real" means not pretending, not putting forth a false image through false action, speech, or thought. "True" means honest, trustworthy, sincere, or accurate. "Integrity" means wholeness, to be in alignment, to have our insides match our outsides, or to walk our talk.

In other words, being authentic means being the person you say you are, speaking honestly the words you mean to speak, and doing what you say you will do. It's knowing who you are and doing *you*, not someone else, or some idea of who you should be, and it's the driving force of an integrated spiritual life. Authenticity is about discovering and acting from our true selves with honesty and sincerity.

Authenticity comes through practices of Attention and Acceptance. If we pay attention and accept ourselves unconditionally, we can stop pretending and allow our vulnerabilities, fears, hopes, and true selves to be seen. We can look in the mirror, and instead of turning away from what we see, own it, and even more than that, walk with it in full integrity, or wholeness. Then, naturally, we will become better people—more honest, humble, transparent, real, and authentic.

WHY IS AUTHENTICITY IMPORTANT?

You have to grow from the inside out. None can teach you. None can make you spiritual. There is no other teacher but your own soul.

SWAMI VIVEKANANDA

One of the highest goals of spiritual inquiry is self-knowledge. It's the first of the Big Three Questions: Who Am I? Every tradition, including the Greek philosophers, calls us to examine ourselves, look inward, unveil ourselves, discover who we truly are as unique manifestations of the Divine, and act from that knowledge. Even psychology emphasizes self-knowledge. As Carl Jung said, "The privilege of a lifetime is to become who you truly are."

Anthony De Mello, an Indian Jesuit priest and psychotherapist, writes about the importance of self-knowledge in his book *Awareness: Conversations with the Masters*: "The great masters tell us that the most important question in the world is: 'Who am I?' Or rather: 'What is I? What is this thing I call I? What is this thing I call self?' You mean you understood everything else in the world and you didn't understand this?"

A wonderful story to illustrate the importance of self-knowledge on the spiritual path is a Hasidic Jewish tale. A young man travels a long distance to visit a famous village Rebbe (spiritual teacher), who asks him, "Why have you come here?"

"To find God," says the eager young man.

"Then you come for nothing," the Rebbe scoffs. "You're wasting your time."

Confused, the young man asks, "But why?"

"Because God is everywhere," the Rebbe waves his arms dismissively.

"Then, tell me, Master," pleads the young man. "Why should I have come?"

"To find yourself."

Authenticity is about self-knowledge or finding yourself—and perhaps finding the Sacred in the process. We must spend the time to get to know ourselves and, through that, come to know the Divine. Whether you find God or not, it's the way to wholeness. Authenticity is the practice of uncovering who you are and acting from your real, true self in the world.

This is not an egoic or self-absorbed "self-knowing." It is knowing your true nature, your unique "beingness." You can't fake authenticity. You can't dictate it. You can't positive affirmation or superficial self-care your way to it. You must get down and dirty and radically real with yourself, others, the world, and the Divine.

American archetypal mythologist Joseph Campbell, best known for his work on *The Hero's Journey* and *The Power of Myth*, called Authenticity "following your *wyrd*." *Wyrd* comes from the Old Norse, meaning "fate" or "destiny." Some translate that as following your "weird" or your "daimon." Eventually, it became the popular saying, "Follow your bliss." I call it listening to and acting upon your "Word," the truth of who you are and what you are here to do. That could include all the definitions above.

In this sense, "Word" is similar to the Greek *logos*, or the logic of the Cosmos, the way the Divine plan manifests in each being. Words are how we define things, and your "Word" is your self-definition, your destiny, your beingness. Your "Word" is unique to you but is not separate from the Divine "Word." "Word" also means truth, as in "You have my word" or "My word is my bond." We are all called to live our divinely given "Word," to know and act with authenticity from our true selves.

On a deeper spiritual level, the one to which De Mello and all the mystics allude, genuine self-knowledge is also a form of self-transcendence. We go from "self" to "selfless" or false self to true self. To know our true, real selves is to know ourselves as indivisible from the Divine. No matter what we call it—God, Spirit, The Eternal I, Buddha-mind, the Dao, or *Sat Nam* in the Hindu tradition—our Word is integral with the Divine Word. As the great 13th-century Buddhist poet Dogen explains:

> To study the Way is to study the Self
> To Study the Self is to forget the Self
> To forget the Self is to be enlightened by all things
> To be enlightened by all things is to remove the barrier
>   between self and other.

In this understanding, unity, oneness, or wholeness equals holiness, and every tradition emphasizes this kind of self-knowledge as the pinnacle of a spiritual life. When we know ourselves truly, we know the Divine. Ibn Arabi, a Sufi mystic, wrote, "When you know yourself, your 'I'ness vanishes, and you know that you and Allah are one and the same."

HOW TO BRING AUTHENTICITY INTO YOUR LIFE

*Awakening is about liberating yourself from
the prison that is the world of the mind and
daring to be here as all that you are.*

LEONARD JACOBSON

Remember the story of The Velveteen Rabbit, who becomes real only when he is truly seen by The Boy, cracked open by his loss, and sheds a tear? What about Pinocchio, the wooden puppet who becomes a real boy when he learns to be honest, humble, and true? These stories, like those from many religious traditions, are parables to remind us that becoming real is a process—and not always a comfortable one—that involves freeing ourselves from our own limiting mental constructs and beliefs, being vulnerable, being honest with ourselves and others, and acting in integrity from that place.

FALSE SELF VS. TRUE SELF

All traditions teach that we have two selves: Our false self and our real self. Sometimes, they are referred to as our egoic self and our True Self, or our "self" with a small "s" and our "Self" with a capital "S." Self-knowledge aims to move from the false self to the real self, from ego to egoless, or to grow up from a small "s" to a big one. To become "real." The True, real, capital "S" Self is our deepest, unchanging nature, soul, or the one we ultimately come to know as indivisible from God, Buddha-mind, Ultimate Reality, or the Dao.

Most of us spend our time in the small "s," egoic, or false self, and there are many ways that appears. Buddhists would say that our small selves (or ego-mind, in Buddhist terminology) are caught in the cycles of *samsara*—endless suffering and rebirth—through ignorance, attachment, and desire. Daoists declare that our small selves are stuck following societal conditioning, rules, or forced action, not in natural alignment with the Dao. Christians, Jews, and Muslims claim our small selves are led astray by greed, lust, anger, and other vices. Indigenous voices tell us that when we forget we are a part of the whole, we are in our small self. All of those are true, but there are even subtler ways we lose touch with our authentic selves.

IDENTITY ISN'T EVERYTHING

Most apparently, we define ourselves with socially and culturally constructed identities, our "I." If we are asked "who" we are, we might answer, "I am ... " followed by Black, white, male, female, or nonbinary, Jewish, Christian, conservative, liberal, mother, father, sister, brother, carpenter, teacher, artist, etc. We might define ourselves by our histories, traumas, successes, or failures—things that happened to us in the past that we decide determine who we are forever.

But identities are only the socially constructed parts of who we are. They are very limiting and keep us small. Though our identities can play an important part in how we belong in communities (or not), we are much more than any labels or identities we give ourselves. So is everyone else. However, if we define ourselves only by our "small self" identities, we must keep propping them up. The ego-self needs support. It needs to prove and defend itself.

For example, if my identity is that I am a smart woman, I might go out of my way to prove that to others. If I am challenged on my "facts," I might get defensive. Or, if my identity is that I am weak and helpless, I might make myself small and allow others to determine my life. These identities and defensive behaviors only serve to reinforce our small, false, egoic selves, limit us and others, and keep us from true self-knowledge.

Every tradition implores us to see ourselves as whole, not parts. To do so, we must stop defining ourselves, others, and the world through isms and ideologies, labels and identities, expectations and boxes of our sociocultural making. If we can see ourselves without these things, we begin to discover our authenticity—and that of others.

REMOVE THE MASK

Beyond our socially constructed identities, we have other ways of living in our small selves. We all put on masks, wanting to appear at times as other than who we are, and thus behave in ways that aren't authentic to our own truth. Many of us are desperate for approval and afraid of the judgment of others, so we sometimes say or do things that go contrary to our deepest needs, values, or true selves to please others or avoid possible rejection or conflict. We aren't being honest with ourselves or others. It's a form of lying.

Some of us make ourselves smaller. Some of us make ourselves bigger. Some of us hide entirely. We don't want to be ourselves, so we try to be someone else, thinking that would be better. We are afraid to show our weakness or our strength. We are afraid that we will not be loved or accepted entirely as we are, even if different from what others expect. This is self-denial and self-rejection, the opposite of self-knowledge or authenticity.

After years of this, we no longer know who we are. As the saying goes, "The mask becomes the man." If we keep these masks on, we will never come to know ourselves authentically. We can never be true, real, or in integrity. Our relationships suffer, our sense of connection and belonging suffer, and our health and feelings of happiness and contentment suffer. Some propose that certain types of depression, anxiety, and addiction stem from a deep, unconscious sense of inauthenticity, that they arise when we aren't living from our truest selves.

We must peel the masks off. It's scary, but Authenticity requires allowing ourselves to be seen and to behave exactly as we are in every moment, as we were created: perfectly imperfect, gloriously messy, and ever-in-process. Part of that is being aware of when we are masking up. We can then choose to take the mask off or put it on if necessary.

The more we practice letting our authentic selves out and being absolutely honest with ourselves and others, the less scary it gets. As one of my dearest and first teachers, Pastor Lillie Mae Bell, used to say, "You come naked to church. God sees right through those fancy clothes." We must be willing to stand honestly naked before the Divine, others, and ourselves.

GET NAKED

To find out who we really are—to stand naked—we must do our work. My teacher, Daoist Abbot Lao Zhi Chang, used to teach the importance of "Finding your innate nature," which is Daoist language for your true self: who you are, unconditioned by your stories, society, and the people around you, your true "beingness," or your "Word." The way we do this involves returning to one's roots. It's a process of reduction.

Like a sculptor chipping away at stone to reveal the figure inside, we don't have to add anything; we must remove everything that isn't "real." We must remove the false masks and limiting identities, the ego-driven needs, defenses, and desires. We must stop lying to ourselves or others and get radically honest without the clothes we wear to disguise ourselves.

The important thing to remember is that Authenticity is not something we have or don't have. It's a practice. We must do our work, and it takes time. We always have the choice to show up as our authentic selves. As Brene Brown says, "Authenticity is a collection of choices we must make every day. It's about the choice to show up and be real. The choice to be honest. The choice to let our true selves be seen."

WHAT IS SELF, ANYWAY?

We've talked a lot about the "self," but what is it? Where is it? How do we even define it? Is it a fixed thing? Many of us define our "self" by our thoughts, as in the famous saying by the philosopher Descartes: "I think, therefore I am." Others define the "self" as the body, the organs, bones, muscles, workings, and appearance of the physical form. Others yet define the "self" by the emotions: I *am* sad, or I *am* happy. We define our "self" as all of this, as well as our stories and identities.

All these things are impermanent. They come and go, and while they are part of our human experience, they cannot be where our real self is located. Again, Jesuit priest and therapist Anthony De Mello explains:

> Listen to this: Am I my thoughts, the thoughts that I am thinking? No. Thoughts come and go; I am not my thoughts. Am I my body? They tell us that millions of cells in our body are changed or are renewed every minute, so that by the end of seven years we don't have a single living cell in our body that was there seven years before. Cells come and go. Cells arise and die. But "I" seems to persist. So am I my body? Evidently not!

When we begin to question what our "self" is, we come up against the realization that we don't know. In our minds, we create a single narrative, the story of "I," in which we are the main character moving unchangingly through our life experiences. If we inquire, we might find that, in fact, there is no "I" that is a single main character, let alone one that doesn't change. After all, are you really the same "I" now that you were when you were six? Or even yesterday?

We discover that what we call "self" isn't a fixed thing but a conglomeration of genetics, environment, experiences, sensations, propensities, and processes. The truth is that we are not a consistent, unchanging "I" or self. Neuroscience has also shown that the self is not consistent and not fixed in a specific part of the brain but is a process of consciousness itself. As Psychologist Carl Rogers explains: "A person is a fluid process, not a fixed and static entity: a flowing river of change, not a block of solid material: a continually changing constellation of potentialities, not a fixed quantity of traits."

YOU ARE GOD

For some, that knowledge can be unsettling. If "I" am not "me," then who am I? Christian, Muslim, and Jewish theology tells us our real "self" is our soul, the part of us directly connected to the Divine. Hindus call it *Atman,* the personal soul connected to *Brahman*, the Ultimate Reality. Buddhists call it Buddha-nature or Buddha Mind and claim it is empty of form. Daoists refer to *Ziran*, our "Such-ness," or *Pu*, or the Uncarved Block, our simple, unconditioned being connected to the Dao, as our "self." Indigenous traditions speak of spirit, and everything has one. In other words, all the wisdom traditions tell us is that there is something besides or beyond our bodies, emotions, stories, and thoughts that is our "True Self," inseparable from the Divine, the All That Is, God, Dao, or Mind.

This, of course, is the deeper spiritual purpose of self-knowledge or Authenticity, in which we discover that the self is a manifestation of the Divine, or, as all the mystics will tell us, one and the same. Our experience of the Divine might determine how we experience our True Selves. However, we can only discover this when we are living authentically from our true selves in the more mundane sense.

FOLLOW YOUR BLISS

According to Sri Ramana Maharshi, one of the great Indian gurus, Hinduism teaches that living from your true, authentic self is *ananda*, or bliss, and it is considered the highest spiritual state of the individual self. This is not a superficial happiness or chasing your desires; it's a deep, abiding sense of joy that comes when you are in alignment with your nature and the world around you and live and act authentically from the very center of your life and being. It is the natural result when you are no longer under the illusion that you must live from your small self. In tune with our real selves, we are truly authentic. This is why Joseph Campbell said, "Follow your bliss!"

When we do follow our bliss or live authentically, there is no disconnection and we are much less apt to behave in ways that are self-destructive or destructive to others or the world around us. In The Bhagavad Gita, Krishna tells Arjuna, "When a man sees that the God in himself is the same God that is in all that is, he hurts not himself by hurting others: then he goes to the highest Path" (13:28).

When we follow our bliss, we might also discover more options for how we can live and act than we had before. We aren't boxed in anymore. We might find that we are drawn to things that surprise us or make choices that seem counter to expected norms. These might be difficult to embrace at first, but when we know they are true to us, we find more courage to go our own path and walk our own way. For many of us, that freedom to finally be wholly, fully ourselves is what we have been craving all along.

LET OTHERS FOLLOW THEIR BLISS, TOO

True self-knowledge also makes us more humble, more open to hearing and seeing the truth of others, and more vulnerable. The True Self has nothing to boast about, nothing to prove, and nothing to defend: that's the ego. Needing to be seen and heard (and agreed with) at all costs isn't the same thing as allowing yourself to be seen and heard truthfully because the cost of not doing so is too painful.

When we allow ourselves to be truly seen and heard, we give others the gift or opportunity to show up authentically, too. They can be honest with us. We might also find that we behave with much more acceptance, compassion, and kindness toward others as a result, and others with us. Not only do we understand how all of us are struggling to follow our bliss, find our authentic selves, or live our "Word," but we are also able to see beneath others' masks and egos with greater compassion. When living authentically in our own truth, we are much more likely to treat others who are living their own truth—to whatever degree—equally valuable, worthy, and deserving of honesty, kindness, and even celebration. After all, if it is OK for me to live my truth, then it is OK for you, too. As Marianne Williamson says:

> Our deepest fear is not that we are inadequate. Our deepest fear is that we are powerful beyond measure. It is our

light, not our darkness that most frightens us. We ask ourselves, "Who am I to be brilliant, gorgeous, talented, fabulous?" Actually, who are you not to be? You are a child of God. Your playing small does not serve the world. There is nothing enlightened about shrinking so that other people won't feel insecure around you. We are all meant to shine, as children do. We were born to make manifest the glory of God that is within us. It's not just in some of us; it's in everyone. And as we let our own light shine, we unconsciously give other people permission to do the same. As we are liberated from our own fear, our presence automatically liberates others.

As we begin to make authentic choices, get glimpses of our true spiritual selves, become more integrated, and come closer to seeing ourselves in our wholeness/holiness, inseparable from the Divine, we begin to see others the same way. We see that we aren't separate from each other. If I am not separate from the Divine, then you are not separate from the Divine, and then I am not separate from you. We are all connected, which is what all traditions teach at their core, and we can all become better people in a better world.

> *When you see all beings in the Self*
> *And the Self in all beings*
> *You fear no one.*
> **ISHA UPANISHAD 6**

REFLECTION QUESTIONS

1. What does Authenticity mean to me?

2. Why is Authenticity important to me?

3. What social identities do I have? How do I let them define me? How do I defend them? Who would I be without them?

4. What masks do I wear? Do I seek approval from others and conceal parts of myself to gain it?

5. What do I lie about to myself or others?

6. How do I make myself small? How do I make myself big?

7. What do I know to be true about myself?

8. How can I show up more honestly, with more integrity?

9. How do I experience myself as indivisible from the Divine?

SUGGESTED PRACTICES

1. Make a list of what you believe to be your true qualities. Where do you see those qualities revealed? Where are they hidden?

2. Can you remember when you were a young child? What were you like? Are you still like that? If not, why not?

3. Take one or two free online psychological assessments, i.e., Briggs-Myers, Human Design, etc. What do they reveal about you? Do you agree?

4. Many traditions suggest silent meditation, solitude, or contemplation for discovering your true self. Choose a technique that helps you listen for what is true for you, and practice.

5. Imagine you have forgotten all your past and history, all the stories. Who are you in this moment without them?

6. Practicing seeing others as trying to follow their "bliss" without judging it. How does that change your experience of them?

4

Benevolence

Benevolence is the characteristic element of humanity

CONFUCIUS

According to Merriam-Webster, Benevolence is marked by the desire for the well-being of self and others and the willingness to extend that desire actively. The Latin roots *bene,* or "good," and *velle,* "to wish," mean wishing others well, wanting the happiness of others, or goodwill.

When goodwill becomes action, it shows up as kindness, charity, mercy, affirmation, patience, forgiveness, humaneness, warmth, friendliness, compassion, ordinary decency, fair play, generosity, and love for self and all beings. Benevolence is considered the primary attribute of the Divine and is our innate, normal state of being when we are not under perceived stress or threat. We humans are naturally kind.

All traditions stress Benevolence, which could be summed up simply as "be kind." But Benevolence doesn't come from the outside; it starts from the inside. It extends from Attention, Acceptance, and Authenticity. If we accept ourselves, others, and the world unconditionally *and* act from our authentic, true selves, we will naturally offer others and the world our goodwill; we will want their well-being, as well as our own. Benevolence shines a light of goodwill on all, regardless of who or what they are.

WHY IS BENEVOLENCE IMPORTANT?

The aim of a spiritual life is to awaken a joyful freedom, a benevolent and compassionate heart in spite of everything.

JACK KORNFIELD

Every tradition talks about the qualities of Benevolence—goodwill, kindness, compassion, mercy, charity—as being the highest of virtues. These qualities and behaviors make living among other beings and the world at large tolerable for everyone; without them, the world is a mean, dark, dangerous, ugly place. In fact, it is only through acts of benevolence that human beings have survived.

In one way or another, in every tradition, we are asked to cultivate our capacity for Benevolence. In most traditions, this appears as moral codes, ethical precepts, rules, or lists of prohibitions, admonitions, and injunctions on how to behave or how not to behave in the hopes of developing an inner sense of "rightness," to ease social relationships, or to avoid Divine punishment. Regardless of how we are taught to be benevolent, the point is that these qualities are considered among the most important virtues we can have.

These are also qualities attributed to the Divine itself, whether as all-merciful, beneficent, compassionate, loving, generous, or kind. When we say, "God is good," we mean God is benevolent (even if it doesn't always appear that way). To align ourselves with the Divine is one goal of spiritual practice, and when we do, Benevolence is the result. Moreover, all traditions teach us that every being is Divine by nature, and thus, not only are we capable of acting as benevolently as the Divine does, but when we see the Divine in others, as well as ourselves, we will want to treat them with goodwill, too.

Christianity, Judaism, and Islam all hold the qualities of love, mercy, charity, forgiveness, compassion, kindness, and the Golden Rule as fundamental and non-negotiable. "Do unto others as you would have them do unto you" or "Don't do to others what is hateful to yourself." In Islam, there are the fundamental tenets of sincerity (*al-ikhlas*), honesty (*al-sidq*), and goodwill (*al-nasihah*). The Torah, the Talmud, the teachings of Jesus, the Bible, the Qur'an, the Hadith, and other texts give us countless instructions, details, and examples of how that will be accomplished. In myriad ways, we are instructed and required to behave with Benevolence—goodwill and kindness—toward others.

In the Hindu and Jain traditions, Benevolence is best described as *ahimsa*, or non-harm, and is one of the highest virtues. While it most often appears in precepts as "Do not kill," the principle of *ahimsa* extends far beyond avoiding causing physical harm. Through our words, thoughts, and actions, we can kill hopes, dreams, ideals, beliefs, and people's spirits, not just their physical beings. It's also not limited to people. Plants, animals, our planet—anything whatsoever can be harmed. *Ahimsa,* then, is non-injury in mind, speech, and action *in any way* toward *any* being.

Compassion is central to Buddhism. After all, the Buddha's teachings were designed to free beings from suffering. Not only does compassion form the basis of the Boddhisattva vows of Mahayana Buddhism, where working to free others from suffering is considered the highest form of loving kindness, but reverence for Avalokiteshvara, the Buddha of Compassion, and Guan Yin, the Goddess of Mercy and Compassion, is also prevalent in Buddhist theology and practice.

Another specifically Buddhist concept of benevolence is *metta*, a Pali word most often translated as loving-kindness but also translated as universal goodwill or loving-friendliness. The concept originates from the historical Buddha's early discourse on immeasurable friendliness, the *Metta Sutta*. Many Buddhists and non-Buddhists practice *metta* meditation. It's a simple practice in which we offer loving kindness or immeasurable friendliness first to ourselves, then to others, then to all beings everywhere.

For Daoists, compassion is considered one of the Three Virtues, but the highest form of benevolence (*ren*) is to allow all beings to be as they naturally are without trying to make them be a certain way. As expressed in the Daode Jing, the Dao has an inherent goodness and is benevolent without sympathy, sentimentality, or external morality by non-preferentially "nourishing life." Daoist scholar Livia Kohn describes it as "transmoral."

In other words, the Dao doesn't act with the *intention* to do "good," which is a social construct, only to do what is appropriate to nourish life. Thus, in following the Dao, humans should practice nourishing life by supporting and allowing the natural processes of people and things to be as they are without interference. That's the ultimate kindness or Benevolence. As my teacher lovingly used to say, "You do you, Baby, and let the Dao do the rest."

Indigenous traditions revere all of life and see all beings—human, plant, animal, and spirit—as members of one big, interconnected family. In practice, that means all beings are treated as kin, with kindness, compassion, and goodwill. It is often said in these traditions,

"What is done to one is done to all." For example, the African word *ubuntu* means "I am what I am because you are who you are." The practice of *ubuntu* means that interconnectedness requires extending humanity to all others. The supreme deities of indigenous religions are also perceived as having the qualities of Benevolence. Pachamama, The Great Spirit, Olodumare, etc., are all described as compassionate, life-supporting deities.

Contemporary psychology also emphasizes qualities of Benevolence for mental health; if we cannot treat ourselves with loving kindness, we will be unable to treat others that way, and vice versa. Moreover, without kindness, we are likely to feel unsafe and thus will act from stress and threat. Psychologists and neurologists have noted that compassion and forgiveness help us move through trauma, and performing acts of kindness for others does wonders for our well-being, physiologically and emotionally. We simply feel better about ourselves and the world around us when we treat others with kindness.

HOW TO BRING BENEVOLENCE INTO YOUR LIFE

Be kind whenever possible. It's always possible.
HIS HOLINESS THE 14TH DALAI LAMA

Poet Maya Angelou has said, "It takes courage to be kind." It does. The world provides us with every opportunity to act with anger, greed, cruelty, aggression, or hatred. It's not easy to resist those urges and instead act with kindness, goodwill, and compassion. To do so requires heart; the root of courage is the Latin, *cor*, or "heart." In our deepest core, our heart, we genuinely desire well-being for ourselves and others.

There are many instructions in all traditions for how to be benevolent: Do not kill, give charity, care for the poor, treat others with respect, forgive transgressions, do not speak ill of others, etc. These are all valuable as ideals or aspirations. Still, rather than creating another list of "shoulds" dictated by an external authority, we need to know that, for the most part, these behaviors are innate to us and that, in most cases, we naturally do these things.

We already have the capacity for Benevolence; we don't have to force it. We only need to explore and address the obstacles that keep us from our natural state of wishing well for others, even when the going gets tough.

WHY CAN'T WE BE NICE?

If our natural state is benevolent, what prevents us from always being kind? Every tradition talks about the things that make us unkind. We are told that greed, attachment, anger, hatred, feelings of scarcity, jealousy, and a whole host of other emotions or impulses prevent us from behaving with goodwill toward others. The desire for power, control, attention, or material wealth, or the fear that we won't get those things, can sometimes make us behave in ways that are not benevolent.

By the same token, if we are tired, hungry, stressed, or in fear, we struggle to be kind. It's difficult to be nice when we feel that we aren't getting what we want or deserve or that the world is against us. But if we are prone to desires, anger, fear, and stress, how do we move from an attitude of ill will to one of goodwill?

SHIFT THE PERSPECTIVE

This is where the practices of Attention, Acceptance, and Authenticity come into play—again. If we pay attention, we will notice that we might have feelings of ill will or are having a hard time being kind in a particular situation. We can, without judgment, acknowledge those feelings and accept them. There is nothing wrong with having moments in which we are simply having a hard time being kind. It's natural. We can also notice that the world — or others — might be having a difficult time. We can accept that without judgment, too. It may not be what we want or like or feel we deserve, but it is what it is. That's step one.

Once we have accepted the situation for what it is without judgment, we shift the perspective from one focused on our own needs and how they aren't being met to seeing everyone's needs and circumstances, too. We expand our field of vision and throw a softening filter on the lens. As expressed in humanistic psychology, we view all people and things with *unconditional positive regard*, including ourselves.

In other words, instead of making it all about us and our frustration, fear, and needs and assuming the worst of others, we step out of our self-centeredness, put ourselves in others' shoes, give people the benefit of the doubt, and recognize without judgment that everyone is simply doing the best they can under the circumstances, including ourselves. This is goodwill.

It is possible to shift the perspective from ill will to goodwill in the moment, to use our practices of Attention, Acceptance, and Authenticity to remove the stress and fear from the situation so that our natural Benevolence can come out. When we refocus the lens away from our own needs and frustrations and give others the benefit of the doubt, our internal attitude shifts, and we will begin to behave in ways that allow Benevolence to happen naturally. The good news is that we can cultivate this practice so that it becomes more common in our daily lives.

THAT LOVING FEELING

An easy way to cultivate our natural Benevolence is to remember what it feels like when someone or something is kind to you. How does a simple smile, thank you, or favor move you? Do you feel happier, less angry, frustrated, or stressed? Can an act of kindness or compassion completely dispel whatever bad mood you were in? Conversely, what does it feel like to receive acts or words of unkindness?

Psychologists and neurologists have proven that kindness releases neuro-chemicals that make us feel safe, loved, peaceful, and happy. This works when someone is kind to you or when you are kind to others. To shift the internal perspective, you don't need to do anything but remember what it feels like to be treated with kindness, receive the well-wishes of others, or treat another with kindness. Your body and mind will automatically move into a state of peacefulness and calm. From that place, you will be more likely to see yourself and others through the benevolent lens and act accordingly. And if that doesn't work, imagine what it feels like to be treated unkindly. Do you want to do that to yourself or another being?

Another good practice for cultivating that loving feeling is the Buddhist *metta*, or loving kindness, meditation, in which you move from wishing yourself happiness and well-being to wishing it for others and then the whole world. We do this through visualization and repetition of the phrases, "May I (you, all beings) be happy. May I (you, all beings) be well. May I (you, all beings) be safe. May I (you, all beings) be peaceful and at ease. May I (you, all beings) be free from suffering." Try this next time you're stuck in the slow checkout line.

In some traditions, focusing on feeling the mercy, blessings, or love of the Divine makes us feel safe, supported, cared for, and peaceful and helps us extend goodwill to others. Simply noticing Benevolence all around us—food, air, sunshine, and other basic goodness—is a good start. Even in the worst of situations, there is some gift we are receiving for nothing. The practice of gratitude extends from this. Acknowledging that the world is always benevolently supporting your well-being, even if it doesn't appear that way in the moment, can have the same effect as an act of kindness from another person.

ENOUGH TO GO AROUND

Another aspect of Divine Benevolence is that there is no limit to it. There isn't only a certain amount of goodwill in the world reserved only for a select few. There is infinite mercy, compassion, love, and kindness available to all. Sometimes, we can forget that, fearing others will get what we want and there won't be enough to go around. Like children fighting over the last cookie, we become fearful that we will lose out. Then we can get mean.

In our culture, it's easy to feel envious of the abundance, success, privilege, wealth, or beauty of others. Spend any time on social media, and you will notice those feelings arise. It's tempting to bad mouth or denigrate those who have what we want, wish for bad things to happen to them, or even physically attack others for what they have. It's hard to be happy for their good fortune when you feel you have the short end of the stick.

But that's what the practice of Benevolence asks us to do. We must recognize that even if someone else has something that we don't, we don't lose anything by wishing them happiness. Their success doesn't diminish ours. There's enough goodness to go around. We don't lose out by having compassion for them or, at the very least, not wishing them harm. In fact, we might gain something: peace of mind.

Many traditions teach us that what goes around comes around.

Whether we call it *karma* or justice, it's the same idea: If you wish others ill or actively harm them, chances are payback will really suck when it comes your turn. On the flip side, if you act benevolently, chances are that others will be kinder, more generous, and more helpful in return. That's not why we are kind or generous or cultivate Benevolence, but it's a nice side effect when it happens.

FORGIVENESS AND MERCY

All traditions teach us that we must meet injustice with forgiveness, unkindness with kindness, treat our enemies with compassion, overlook the failures of others, turn the other cheek, and so forth. In fact, in all traditions, mercy and forgiveness for those who behave in ways that are hurtful to others are the hallmarks of a compassionate, loving, kind Divine. It's another one of the aspects of Divine Benevolence and something we can embody as well.

It's not easy to offer forgiveness or mercy when you're feeling hurt, but an attitude of Benevolence requires that we find some place in our hearts where we can wish the other well, even if their behavior toward us was hurtful. In this case, forgiveness and mercy can simply be letting go of our desire to hurt them back so as not to cause more harm. Just as we discussed in Acceptance, we don't have to like what they did, we don't have to condone it, we don't have to allow it, and we don't even have to forgive the behavior, but we need to remember that the person and the behavior are separate. We see the Divine in the other, even if they behave badly. *Namaste.* The Divine in me sees the Divine in you.

Even if we cannot forgive the behavior, we can forgive and offer mercy to the person. We can treat them with compassion and kindness by shifting our perspective to positive regard, or what a teacher of mine called "Holy Vision," and recognize they were doing the best they could under the circumstances. If they could have done better, they would have. From that place, at the very least, we can offer compassion and the wish that the causes of the pain, fear, or suffering that made the person behave in such a way be removed for their well-being. That's simple mercy. That's forgiveness. That's Benevolence.

The same can be said for us. Though we strive to behave with kindness and benevolence, we don't always do it. We are human, and there is no way we will ever be 100 percent benevolent all the time. Even God knows we will slip up and offers mercy. We can learn to offer ourselves the same forgiveness and mercy. We can see ourselves through Holy Vision and be kind toward ourselves when we aren't as perfectly benevolent as the Divine.

BE KIND TO YOURSELF

As we said earlier, it's difficult to be kind when you are stressed or fearful. It can be challenging to be kind or benevolent when you are tired, hungry, sick, in physical or emotional pain, overworked, dehydrated, or burnt out. When we haven't been able to get our basic physical and emotional needs met, we tend to be snappy, ill-willed, or even violent. It's not an excuse; it's a reality. The lower your Foundations are, the harder it is.

Self-care is one of the best ways to further your cultivation of Benevolence. This isn't the self-indulgent form of "self-care," but the necessary one. It's being kind to yourself. Paying attention to your physical and emotional needs, noticing when your tank is getting low, your thread is getting short, or your patience is wearing thin. Stopping. Pausing. Eating healthy food. Sleeping. Resting. Playing. Connecting with other people in positive ways. These are all forms of self-kindness necessary for an attitude that promotes goodwill toward self and others.

It's easier to want the well-being of others when your own well-being is being supported. The same is true in reverse; maybe the other person having a hard time being kind is just hangry, didn't sleep well last night, or having a bad day. We don't always know the burdens and struggles of one another. Perhaps a good meal, a kind word, or a little R&R could help them feel and act more benevolently, too.

The extension of self-kindness and self-care is self-compassion. Having compassion for others as they struggle to do their best is sometimes easier than turning that compassion toward ourselves. We tend to have high expectations for ourselves and a lot of "shoulds." However, we all make mistakes, have bad days, strive to do the best we can under the circumstances, and sometimes, we slip up. Giving yourself the benefit of the doubt and seeing yourself with unconditional positive regard is critical.

Forgiving yourself or not beating yourself up for not being perfect all the time is a profound form of Benevolence. As Kristin Neff, author of *Fierce Self-Compassion,* says, "If we're going to bring justice to an inequitable society, we'll need to make sure that our compassion is directed toward ourselves as much as toward others."

As you practice cultivating a benevolent attitude, stay mindful of what you might need to care for yourself. By supporting or encouraging others' needs to eat, sleep, rest, relax, play, be self-compassionate, or just take a little break, we might also help them cultivate Benevolence.

RANDOM ACTS OF KINDNESS

Aldous Huxley, author of *The Perennial Wisdom*, said near the end of his life, "It's a bit embarrassing to have been concerned with the human problem all one's life and find at the end that one has no more to offer by way of advice than 'try to be a little kinder.'" My own teacher had another way of saying the same thing: "Try not to be a jerk." If there is one simple way to cultivate Benevolence, it's to try to be kind to yourself and others in any way possible without expectation.

There is a popular bumper sticker that reads, "Practice Random Acts of Kindness." It's a good instruction and echoes the Daode Jing teaching: "The highest benevolence is without purpose." Simply being kind to another person in an unmediated way—without expectation of reward—can physiologically, psychologically, and spiritually transform you and the world. We already do it. Just look around. Without the unmediated acts of kindness that are happening everywhere, all the time, we probably wouldn't survive.

Any time we act with kindness or compassion in any small way—and are doing so not because we seek reward or to manipulate—we are cultivating Benevolence. When we genuinely wish another person "Have a good day" or help someone struggling to cross a busy street because it's the appropriate thing to do in that moment, we are making the world a little kinder. Some say no act of kindness is small, as the effects ripple out. You never know how something random and nice can change someone's life or the world. It certainly doesn't hurt. As Jack Kerouac said, "Practice kindness all day to everybody, and you will realize you're already in heaven now."

BE THE CHANGE

Mahatma Gandhi, who adapted the principle of *ahimsa* to non-violent resistance, said, "Be the change you want to see in the world." In other words, it doesn't do to criticize the world for being unkind if we aren't willing to start being kind ourselves. If we want the world to be a kinder, more benevolent place, it must start with us.

It's important that we explore where and how we cause harm to ourselves, others, and the world around us and become mindful of what we can do differently. Before we speak or act, we must ask ourselves: "Is it true (authentic or honest)? Is it kind? Is it necessary? Could it cause harm? Is it coming from fear or expectation? What is the kindest, most benevolent, or compassionate thing to do or say in this situation?"

Sometimes, despite our best intentions to be kind, something we say or do causes harm we didn't expect. As the old saying goes, "The road to hell is paved with good intentions." We can't always know all the downstream effects of our actions, but we can try to be mindful of our intentions and the possible results—and apologize if we miscalculated.

We must also remember that kindness and doing "good" are two different things. When we think we are doing "good," we may be inadvertently causing harm by imposing our version of "good" on someone else. What one person thinks is best may not be best for another. Spiritual teacher Alan Cohen reminds us, "To think you know what is best for another person is an industrial-strength ego trip."

Moreover, acting in a non-harmful way doesn't always look like what we think it should. We might have to say "No" to something someone wants if it could cause them or others harm, which might make them angry or upset. For example, if a friend has had too much to drink and insists on driving, we might need to take their car keys and offer to drive them home so they don't hurt themselves or others. This might make them angry, but it's in everyone's best interest. In another context, burning parts of a forest might be necessary to help it thrive. Some might say doing so harms the trees, plants, and animals, but it might be for the best long-term well-being of all if done responsibly.

Sometimes, the least harmful thing might be to do or say nothing. My grandmother used to instruct me, "If you can't say something kind, don't say anything at all." Sometimes, the best action is no action. We may not have any option that won't cause harm in a situation, so we may need to sit on our hands or keep our mouths shut until there's a better, more appropriate choice. That could be the least harmful thing to do.

On a larger social and political level, this consideration for kindness and non-harm takes on even more importance. These days, when opinions and beliefs about how the world should be are waved like battle flags, it's critical to consider if what we think is "good," "right," or "non-harmful" truly is. We must ask if our need to be right or do "good" is stronger than our need to be kind. If it is, we must let go of the need to be good or right and just be kind. Or maybe we can explore a way to be good, right, *and* kind at the same time.

Baruch Spinoza, a Jewish philosopher, once said, "Peace is not an absence of war; it is a virtue, a state of mind, a disposition for benevolence, confidence, justice." If we meet anger, righteousness, ill will, and injustice with more anger, righteousness, ill will, and injustice, are we not adding to the lack of kindness in the world? Is that a "disposition for benevolence" or justice? Will it help us achieve a kinder, more peaceful world? Is wishing goodwill only to those who agree with us the same as wishing goodwill to all?

Though it may be our natural state, true Benevolence isn't just about what makes you feel good or gives you the warm fuzzies. Kindness is not only about what makes you feel safe and comfortable.

Sometimes, we might have to extend ourselves beyond what we normally do. According to activist and writer Jenny Justice, "Kindness is about making others feel good and have good even if, even when, it might push you out of your comfort zone. Kindness is a moral pull rooted in deep empathy. Kindness is striving for justice in every interaction."

If we trust the wisdom of all traditions, we can see that Benevolence is not neutral; it's a definite leaning in to support the well-being of others, even if it is not easy or comfortable. Benevolence requires us to find a way to promote justice while still offering goodwill toward others, no matter what they might believe or do. After all, if we cannot meet conflict and difference with kindness, mercy, and goodwill, how can we ever expect to build a better world?

Simple kindness to one's self and all that lives is
the most powerful transformational force of all.

DR. DAVID R. HAWKINS

REFLECTION QUESTIONS

1. What does Benevolence mean to me?

2. Why is Benevolence important to me?

3. What prevents me from being benevolent?

4. What do I experience when someone is kind to me? What does kindness feel like?

5. What do I experience when someone is unkind to me? What does it feel like when I am unkind to myself?

6. How can I be kinder and more benevolent to myself?

7. How can I be kinder and more benevolent to others?

8. Does my benevolence extend to all beings? In what ways can I be kinder to the non-human?

9. Do I notice the Benevolence in the world around me?

10. How can I practice Benevolence in my workplace? In the world?

SUGGESTED PRACTICES

1. Research the concepts and teachings of Benevolence in different traditions. Do any of them feel important for you to practice? Are there any you already practice? Any you would like to add?

2. Take care of your Foundations. Notice when you are tired, hungry, stressed, or anxious, and it is harder to be kind. Make a point to eat, sleep, rest, relax, play, connect with others, take a break, and get into nature. Do whatever you need to do to stay stress-free to help you access your natural state of Benevolence.

3. Practicing *metta* meditation daily is a good practice for cultivating the capacity for benevolence. There are lots of resources to teach you how to do this.

4. Practice random acts of kindness. At any opportunity, try to do something kind for another. It doesn't have to be a grand gesture; even a smile is an act of kindness. Of course, if the kindest thing would take more than a smile, try to do that.

5. Notice the Benevolence in the world around you. Notice that the world is perfectly tuned to support life—air, sunshine, food—and your life. Consider that even if it doesn't always look that way, the world offers kindness everywhere.

6. In any situation, ask: How can I be kinder, more compassionate, or more benevolent? What is the kindest, least harmful thing to do or say? Accept that the answer may be nothing or look differently than you thought.

5

Balance

Let us be in harmony in our intention,
in harmony in our hearts
in harmony in our minds
that we may live in concord.

RIG VEDA X

In every tradition, there are teachings about balance and harmony. Early theology was profoundly aware of—and insistent on—a balanced cosmos, or the Natural Law of the universe, which creates a harmonious whole. From the Vedas to the Bible, indigenous teachings to Buddhist sutras, we are told that living in balance, harmony, equilibrium, and equanimity with ourselves, others, and the world around us is the basis of spiritual life; it creates peace, well-being, and allows all beings to thrive.

Being out of balance or in disharmony creates pain, suffering, and, some would say, evil. Modern psychology and medicine also emphasize balance for physical, mental, and emotional health, with imbalance being the cause of illness and disease. Even modern physicists and biologists tell us that the Cosmos and life itself are exquisitely balanced, a holistic, harmonious, unified symphony of parts.

Balance arises naturally when we pay attention, accept what is, and act from our true selves with Benevolence. When we are in balance and harmony, life flows; we are content, peaceful, and able to handle what comes at us. Balance and harmony don't mean that everything is flat or the same; like harmony in music, there is an easeful relationship between the different parts.

In many ways, Balance is finding the fulcrum between what appear to be opposites: it's a movement between what is too much or not enough. Janine M. Benyus, creator of Biomimicry, calls it "dynamic non-equilibrium," and it's a spectrum, not an either/or. Sometimes, the world feels out of balance from our viewpoint, but it might not be from a different one.

Sometimes, we are out of balance, or at one end or another, and that's normal; we are often thrown off balance by our thoughts, emotions, others, and the world around us. However, our natural tendency is toward the center of the spectrum, or Balance. Our task is to strive for balance and harmony in ourselves, others, and the world, not always to achieve it.

WHY IS BALANCE IMPORTANT?

He who lives in harmony with himself
lives in harmony with the universe.
MARCUS AURELIUS

From the beginning of human history, balance and harmony with self, others, and the natural world was imperative to survival. Our ancestors understood the delicate balancing act required for humans to co-exist with each other and the world around them. Careful attention to the use of resources, ways of behaving toward other humans and animals, and relationships with spirits or deities perceived to affect human fate were all part of early human life.

For that reason, indigenous teachings are perhaps the most insistent upon balance and harmony. All indigenous traditions are defined by ways to maintain harmony and balance between humans and the natural world—seeing the universe as a holistic, interconnected system and balancing our part in it. Hopi elder Thomas Banyacaya explains, "Let us live in peace and harmony to keep the land and all life in balance."

Shamanic practices, spirit medicine, offerings, and other rituals from Indigenous peoples all seek to maintain that balance. For example, the Andean/Q'ero practice of *Ayni*, or Reciprocity, is designed to maintain the balance between heaven and earth, humans and the natural world, and humans and the Divine through behavior, prayer, and ritual.

The concepts of balance and harmony are also key to Daoism. The Daoist image of the Yin/Yang, perhaps the most well-known symbol of balance and harmony, clearly illustrates how everything in the Cosmos is in a constant state of balance. And, as the Daode Jing repeatedly emphasizes, our goal is to live in harmony, or flow, with the ever-changing Dao. Thus, much of Daoist practice is geared toward balance and harmony, both within the body and mind of the practitioner and in the world at large. Even Traditional Chinese Medicine, which partly comes from Daoist teachings, focuses on bringing the various energies of the body into harmony and balance to cure or prevent illness.

The Vedas, the Upanishads, and the Bhagavad Gita of the Hindu tradition teach harmony and balance. In fact, the practice of yoga itself is about creating balance, harmony, and mental equilibrium. Patanjali's *Yoga Sutras* state, *"Yogas Chitta Vritti Nirodhah,"* which translates to "Yoga stills the fluctuations of the mind." It is by balancing the mind that peace and harmony are attained. Likewise, the teachings of the *gunas*, or the subtle qualities evident in all of nature, tell us that *Sattva* is the quality of balance, or the primordial sense of harmony and equanimity in the Cosmos and our own consciousness. As the state of balance, *Sattva* is responsible for all true health and healing. Health is maintained by Sattvic living, which is living in harmony with nature and our inner self.

For Buddhists, the Middle Way is a primary teaching on balance and harmony. Having observed that the extreme ascetic practices of some spiritual teachings brought no more freedom from suffering than the indulgences of his princely life, The Buddha taught that moderation in all things was the key to health, cessation of suffering, and happiness. Mental equanimity and equilibrium are also central to Buddhist teachings. *Upekkha* is a Pali word for equanimity and is cited many times in the sutras when talking about mental balance. Buddhist meditation techniques, like Hindu and Daoist ones, are designed to still the fluctuations of the mind and bring the meditator into a state of equanimity and balance.

Islam also teaches harmony and moderation, closely related to balance (*tawazun*) and justice (*'adl*), as justice implies balancing rights and duties and setting everything in its rightful place. The moderate, just, and correct action in any given situation often involves balancing various concerns and seeking the middle ground between them. The Prophet Mohammed (PBUH) also taught that Muslims should balance their spiritual life with their home life. Even in prayer, balance and moderation were extolled: Do not recite too loudly in your prayer nor too softly, but seek a way between them (Surat Al-Isra 17:110).

In the Old and New Testaments, we are repeatedly told that living in harmony with others is vital. In fact, many of the Ten Commandments remind us to live in harmony with others and the world around us. "Do not kill" or "Respect your parents" are all teachings about maintaining harmony and balance. The Bible tells us that those who live in peace, unity, and harmony with others are beloved by God. It is taught, "If possible, so far as it depends on you, live peaceably with all" (Romans 12:18). *Halakha*, or Jewish Law, offers many legal guidelines to maintain balance with self, others, and even the earth. For example, keeping the Sabbath helps people maintain mental and physical health, and leaving fields fallow every seventh year so they can return to a healthy balance is encoded in the law!

Psychology and medicine both stress the importance of balance and harmony for health and well-being. Whether eating a balanced diet, getting a moderate amount of exercise, reducing stress, taking time for ourselves, or balancing work with rest and play, it's evident that balance is the key to our physical and mental health.

The hard sciences also talk about the importance of balance. Not only do physicists and cosmologists understand the inherent harmony of the Cosmos on all levels, but biologists stress that life itself is a delicate balance, and for life to exist at all, that balance must be maintained. Today, as our environment teeters on the edge of destruction, we can see the devastating effects caused by imbalance with the natural world.

HOW TO BRING BALANCE INTO YOUR LIFE

*Happiness is when what you think, what you
say, and what you do are in harmony.*

MAHATMA GANDHI

Maintaining Balance is a balancing act. When we start to explore balance and harmony, we find that every aspect of our lives—our minds, our bodies, our work, our spiritual practice, our relationships, our environment, etc.—requires balance for us to be healthy, happy, thriving, and spiritually harmonious. When we align ourselves with the balance and harmony found in the Cosmos, we, too, become balanced.

However, we are often not in balance, and equilibrium is not static. Like the world itself, it's a constant dance along a spectrum between what seem to be opposites. We are very easily thrown into a state of imbalance, even momentarily. Therefore, we are constantly adjusting, fine-tuning, and bringing ourselves back into balance again.

With practice, we are out of balance less often. Balance doesn't mean it's "all good." We need to be in balance with imbalance, as well. It's OK to be out of balance sometimes and sometimes even necessary, but the idea is to work toward less extreme imbalances. Keeping ourselves in Balance enables us to be in greater harmony with others and the world and vice versa.

WORK/LIFE

In our 24/7/365 culture, work is all-consuming. Being "busy" is considered a virtue; a ten-hour workday is common, and many people must work seven days a week just to make ends meet. If we aren't "busy," we feel like we are somehow failing. Many of us fear being viewed as lazy or somehow not moving forward in our lives or careers if we aren't working all the time, even to our detriment. Burnout and stress-related illnesses are the result. The work/life balance, or the balance between one aspect of our lives and others, like parenting/coupling or solitude/togetherness, is the challenge.

We know that all work and no play creates stress, destroys relationships and health, and makes our lives and communities dangerously imbalanced. Our ancestors warned us about this when they commanded, "Keep the Sabbath." Taking a day of rest from work—however we define it—is imperative to maintaining balance in our bodies, minds, and spirits. After all, according to Genesis, even God rested after all that work of creating the Universe! Daoism teaches us that action comes from rest; they must alternate. One cannot always be in action—even indigenous traditions built in times for rest through celebrations and feasts.

Not everyone can afford a day of rest, but we can intentionally make time every day to reconnect with our loved ones, enjoy a hobby or some outside time, or for spiritual practice. That's why the Benedictines and many other monastic traditions have a set schedule to ensure that all the important activities of life get the time they need. There is a time for prayer, work, study, and rest. We need to keep all the parts of our lives moving in harmony. Too much of any one activity or too little of another will cause imbalance.

Many traditions discuss the importance of beginning and ending the day in intentional quiet, study, or practice to keep our days from running away. Some people set aside a "Sabbath hour" each day, or one day a month, to disconnect from the phone or computer and spend time doing things they enjoy with people they enjoy, simply resting or eating well.

Creating a balanced life is our work. As contemporary Hindu teacher Sadhguru says, "There is no such thing as work-life balance—it is all life. The balance is in you." Even if you love your work and are passionate about what you do, take the time to explore where your work life and the rest of your life might be out of balance. The same applies to parenting/coupling, solitude/togetherness, or any other dichotomy in life activities that seem out of balance. Explore ways to bring moderation and a "middle way" to your life.

BALANCE THE MIND

Our minds get us into trouble. As we discussed in Attention, all too often, we get stuck in the contents of our minds, and our thoughts run away like wild horses. The myriad mundane concerns, the stories we tell ourselves, our beliefs, or our worries and fears create disharmony and imbalance and keep us from being content, peaceful, and clear. The balance between our discursive mind—the mind always thinking and figuring things out—and our receptive mind—the one that rests in awareness—is at issue.

For this reason, all traditions emphasize balancing the mind through practices such as meditation, silent prayer, and contemplation. As we learned in our exploration of Attention, without consciously stopping, taking a break, or slowing down our minds, we not only miss most of the present moment and thus the experience of wonder, awe, and divinity in everything, but we aren't able to balance or bring harmony to our lives.

On a spiritual level, bringing balance to the mind is the way toward deeper spiritual realization. The mystics in all traditions emphasize the importance of resting the mind as the means of hearing the voice of God, connecting to the Dao, or realizing Buddha-nature. You can't hear the Divine if your mind is too noisy with other things. As we explore Balance, notice if your mind is too busy in the mundane world to hear that "still, small voice within," and consider ways you might bring more balance to your mind.

THE EMOTIONAL ROLLERCOASTER

Humans can make a real mess of things if we let our emotions get the better of us. Therefore, in all traditions, extreme emotions are considered detrimental to harmony and balance, and many teachings instruct us to harness those intense feelings for our and others' benefit. Even psychology emphasizes the need to let strong emotions settle before acting, and the ability to self-regulate our emotions is a hallmark of mental health.

This isn't to say that we must suppress our legitimate, natural emotions of anger, grief, fear, joy, ecstasy, love, or true passion (in fact, we can celebrate those emotions), but we must learn not to let our passions or desires run riot. There is a balance between attending to our emotional life and letting it run the show. Once again, what appears to be a game of opposites is really a spectrum of possibilities.

Our legitimate emotions are healthy; they arise naturally from circumstances, not from the stories we tell ourselves. But when we find ourselves overcome by our emotions in ways that are detrimental to our sense of balance or harmony, we might need to give ourselves a "time out." Take a walk, take a break, take a bath. Take a few minutes to settle. Meditate. Talk to a friend or counselor.

If we don't control our extreme emotions, not only are we out of balance, but chances are that whatever we say or do will cause further imbalance and disharmony for ourselves and others. If your emotions are running high, consider what practices you might need to help you calm down and let things settle so your emotions are more balanced.

EMBODIED BALANCE

How we relate to our body informs part of every tradition. In some traditions, there appears to be a split between the body and soul, or spirit. While some emphasize body negation or physical asceticism as a means of purification, transcendence, or purgation, at the mystical root of all traditions, the body and spirit are not separate, and the body is honored as one of the means through which we attain spiritual enlightenment.

Through the body itself, we experience life; thus, the body is considered holy, a tabernacle for the Divine incarnate, or the soul. As 13th Century German monk, theologian, and mystic Meister Eckhart said, "The soul loves the body." We are embodied beings: body, mind, and spirit.

Our ancestors knew that the body and mind were intimately related: The teachings of many indigenous traditions say that if our bodies are out of balance, our minds (and the world around us) will be, too. There is a resonance between them. More recently, science has corroborated these findings. Neuroscientists continually discover that the body *is* the mind for all intents and purposes, and physicians note that the mind can heal the body on its own. All agree that without balance in the body, there will be illness or disease, whether physical, psychological, or spiritual.

For these reasons and more, many traditions have body-balancing practices, including dietary, movement, sexual, or otherwise. The Eastern traditions have been most insistent on these types of practices. Yoga, t'ai chi, qigong, and many martial arts are body/mind practices. Ayurveda and Traditional Chinese Medicine are medical systems designed to harmonize the body and maintain balance. Indigenous traditions also have many body-balancing practices, from herbalism to shamanic ceremonies.

The Western traditions, most often considered body-negating, also have body-based practices. Judaism and Islam have dietary and physical cleanliness practices designed to maintain health. The various prayer postures of *salat*, or Islamic prayer, like yoga, are forms of body/mind balancing, and the whirling of the Sufi dervishes use dance and movement to bring the body and spirit together. Jews *daven*, or rock while praying, which is a body/mind balancing practice, and even the chanting and choral singing of Christian worship have a body/mind balancing effect.

Even without ritual forms of body balancing, we can bring balance to our bodies. Taking a walk, a nap, a break, or a bath helps us balance and come into harmony. At the minimum, eating healthy food, drinking clean water, getting outside, being less sedentary, sleeping, and connecting to others in healthy ways go a long way toward feeling balanced and harmonious.

More is not better when it comes to the body. If we overdo it, we throw the body out of balance. If we party too hard too often or hit those killer workouts hard every day, the body—and consequently the mind—will suffer. We don't need four hours of yoga every day to be in balance, nor do we need to be hyper-obsessive and prohibitive about our diet or wellness (unless we are ill and need to regain balance). That's not moderation. That's not Balance. There can be too much of a good thing, and then it's no longer good.

THE PLEASURE PRINCIPLE

Pleasure in all forms, as experienced through our bodies and minds, is also healthy and natural. Enjoyment of food and drink, music and dancing, physical activity, or sensuality is what the Greeks called *eros,* or the love of life. In theological terms, it is akin to the full-bodied pleasure the Divine experiences through unity with creation (or creation with the Divine). The Bible and other sacred literature often describe union with the Divine in erotic terms. Rumi's love poems are about union with the Divine, and the Song of Songs is as erotic as it gets! But this *eros* isn't sexual. It's deeper than that.

At the purest level, *eros* is a love for truth, beauty, and goodness, which calls someone outside of themselves into union with another. It is truly the love of all of life and the physical sensations that bring us into contact with aliveness. Christian theologian Matthew Fox encourages us to "savor" life as a means of connecting to the Divine, including our bodies and sexuality. Interestingly, the word "enjoy" was supposedly coined by a female Christian mystic, Julian of Norwich, who likened it to finding deep, erotic pleasure in all of God's creation.

Every tradition encourages us to enjoy the sweet blessings—the gifts—of being alive in a body. But as with everything, a little goes a long way. Hedonism isn't balanced, and neither is denial. Fully enjoy what you enjoy as the gift of life, even if it's an ecstatic pleasure, but keep it in balance.

The same is true for our sexuality. Both condemned and celebrated throughout human history, at the mystical root of all traditions, our sexuality—the natural expression of our creative energy and desire to merge—is exalted, in balance, and healthy. Former Catholic monk Thomas Moore has written extensively on the spirituality of sex, insisting that there are healthy ways to bring our spiritual lives and sex together simply by applying some of the principles of a spiritual life, such as ethics, community, contemplation, generosity, prayer, and ecstasy.

Some traditions—especially in monastic or priestly sects—demand celibacy or abstinence at times to focus on spiritual practice, while other traditions have sex-based practices, like Tantric Buddhism or the Daoist Bedchamber Arts, which explore sexuality as a means of understanding Divine union and creativity. But we don't have to go to those extremes to put sex in its proper spiritual place as something to enjoy and celebrate. It might seem contradictory, but at their core, all traditions teach respect for healthy, balanced, sexual expression not only as a human need but as a Divine one.

WOBBLY FOUNDATIONS

Whether we are talking about balancing the mind, emotions, body, or life, they all have one thing in common: they need a strong foundation. Just as we discussed in Benevolence, our Foundations—eating, hydrating, sleeping, resting, relaxing, connecting, and playing—are required for us to be our best selves. Without taking care to be balanced in our basic physical and emotional needs, we won't have the mental or physical ability for our spiritual practice or even to enjoy life.

Most of us are trying to care for our Foundations, but it's not always easy. Sometimes, it's effortless, but on other days, we are way off balance. We get wobbly. However, if we make care of our Foundations a priority and are consistently attentive to them, we find we are less likely to get to that point of imbalance in the first place. That's the long-term goal. We want to maintain equilibrium more often so that we are better able to deal with the stresses of life with equanimity.

On a spiritual level, caring for our Foundations also means that we have energy for our spiritual practices, energy to give to others, and are more likely to stay in balance in other areas of our lives. We are also better able to tap into and experience the harmony and balance all around us, perhaps recognizing that it is both our nature and the nature of the Divine to be in harmony and balance.

WHY CAN'T WE ALL JUST GET ALONG?

We are socially embedded beings. Thus, all traditions are emphatic about being in harmony with our fellow humans. Most teachings, commandments, and precepts are about how to behave well with others so that everyone can be healthy, happy, and safe. Justice, compassion, fairness, and respect are all concepts that point toward harmony with others and come from our spiritual traditions.

In a related cosmos, injustice is an imbalance in the cosmic order. Likewise, the balance between self and self-less, pointed to in every tradition, is necessary for harmonious relations. If we only think of ourselves and not others, we are destined for trouble. And vice versa. Introspection has its place, but how our introspection helps us relate more harmoniously to others is the point.

Balance and harmony with others also flow directly from some of the other Ten Words, especially Acceptance, Authenticity, and Benevolence. If we truly want what's best for our brothers and sisters and act from that desire authentically with Attention and Acceptance, then we will naturally get along better with others. It becomes less of a challenge to play nicely.

Of course, it's not always that easy. Especially these days, when passions and tensions are running high, it's challenging to find ways to co-exist and thrive together. Again, if we take care of our own Foundations and consider the teachings of fairness, respect, kindness, and compassion, we might find that it is easier to walk in equilibrium and harmony with others, trusting that together we will find that balance we so desire and need.

WE ARE THE WORLD

Taking our cue from the fundamental teachings of every tradition, but especially our indigenous brothers and sisters, it's critical that balance and harmony include our relationship with all beings and the planet around us. This cosmic awareness believes that the Cosmos itself is the Divine. Most of us are now aware that our planet and the plants and animals on it are in grave danger due to climate change and our human consumption patterns. Things are terribly imbalanced and getting worse.

If we—and our fellow beings of all kinds—have any hope of surviving, we humans must learn, once again, to live in harmony not only with each other but with all species and the planet itself. As Sun Bear, a Chippewa elder, has said, "I do not think the measure of a civilization is how tall its buildings of concrete are, but rather how well its people have learned to relate to their environment and fellow man."

All our spiritual traditions teach us that we need to be more conscious of how we live in relationship to our planet and her other citizens. There is a balance between our desires and the rights and needs of other beings, a natural order to the universe that is upset if any part of it is imbalanced. We are an integral part of that balance. All traditions teach that greed and overconsumption are harmful. These days, that means becoming more aware of our consumption patterns, how we use and share resources, or what businesses, institutions, actions, or governments we support, and making changes to bring about a greater balance. It might mean we need to simplify our lives and our possessions.

At the same time, we must take care to balance our concerns and fears for the planet and her citizens with our belief and trust that things can change. If we find ourselves in deep despair or anger, we are imbalanced and likely to act from fear and worry. Likewise, if we are naively optimistic or in denial about realities, we might miss opportunities to come into better balance with our natural environment. There is a happy medium, a realistically hopeful middle way for which we can strive.

HEAD IN THE CLOUDS, FEET ON THE GROUND

Sometimes, we look at life and the world around us and want to escape it. In fact, some traditions are so focused on transcendence or the "after-life" of heavenly delights that they forget about this one we are living now. On the other hand, many traditions emphasize that we live in two worlds. Our earthly one and our heavenly one, matter and spirit, are indivisibly related. In other words, we are spiritual beings having an earthly experience. Therefore, we are responsible for dealing with both the reality of life here *and* the Ultimate Reality. It's not spiritual or material; it's both.

As we consider creating a balance between our spiritual and material lives, we seek a middle way in which our spiritual lives are not separated or elevated above our mundane ones but deeply embodied and embedded in our everyday lives in a balanced way. We can no longer afford to turn away from the world through forms of spiritual escapism or spiritual bypassing, using our spirituality to negate, gloss, or ignore real-world "stuff." Nor can we afford to shun the spiritual for the purely material.

We must use our spiritual practice to enhance and enrich our messy everyday lives. My teacher used to say, "The boulder *is* the path!" In other words, our spiritual path is only walked through the obstacles of our daily lives. That's how we learn, grow, and become more spiritually centered. In that way, our spiritual life and our mundane life aren't separate; we live in two worlds, but they are in such harmony and balance as to be in unity.

Ultimately, that's the highest form of Balance: Unity. Like music. When two voices or instruments are playing in harmony, the effect is of balance and wholeness. It's all one piece of music with different parts that play well together. If we look again at the yin/yang symbol, we will notice that while two opposing sides are swirling around one another in a dance of balance and harmony, they are enclosed in a single circle. Unity in balance. The Ouroboros is also a symbol of balance in unity of the cycles of creation and destruction. Not surprisingly, that's also how many traditions and mystics describe the Divine—as a unified, balanced, harmonious whole. If we want to live in harmony and unity with the Divine Balance, balance with all of life is the key.

So divinely is the world organized that every one of us,
in our place and time, is in balance with everything else.
JOHANN WOLFGANG VON GOETHE

REFLECTION QUESTIONS

1. What does Balance mean to me?

2. Why is Balance important to me?

3. What prevents me from being in Balance?

4. What do I experience when I am in Balance?

5. What do I experience when I am out of Balance?

6. What parts of my work/life are out of balance? How can I bring them into balance?

7. Is my mind too busy? Do I give my mind rest or time to listen to my inner voice?

8. Are my emotions out of balance? How can I bring my emotions in line?

9. Is my body in balance? What can I do to bring more balance and harmony to my physical being?

10. Where are my relationships with others imbalanced? How can I bring balance into my relationship with the others?

11. How can I be in greater balance and harmony with the natural world? With other beings?

SUGGESTED PRACTICES

1. Try a form of Sabbath. Maybe it's a whole day or just a few hours. Try a weekly Device Sabbath to balance our modern dependency on phones, information, and connection.

2. If your work or distractions are consuming your life, set limits.

3. Take time out to settle emotions before speaking or acting.

4. Try quiet sitting or silent prayer. Take a few minutes each day to sit quietly, let thoughts and emotions dissipate naturally, and allow the mind to rest.

5. Explore yoga, t'ai chi, qigong, or other mind/body practices.

6. Eat a healthy diet. Hydrate. Rest. Relax. Play. Sleep. Connect with others.

7. Explore your consumption patterns. Investigate what you really need to buy or own. Try a week without buying anything other than absolute necessities. Explore simplicity.

8. Spend time in nature to discover how the natural world operates in harmony.

Contemplation

Contemplation is learning to receive.
Learning to listen.
MATTHEW FOX

ontemplation is the higher octave of Attention. It is the turning of our attention to that which is both deeply within and beyond ourselves, toward the bigger picture, the whole, or the Divine, with the purpose of developing a connection to or understanding of that in some way. Characterized by the *intentional* cultivation of interior silence, stillness, receptivity, unknowing, and a willingness to enter darkness or mystery, Contemplation is the necessary component of a spiritual life with depth and purpose.

Unlike first five Ten Words, Contemplation is not an inquiry into our psychology or behavior. It's asking the deeper questions: Who am I at my most authentic level? What is Reality? What do I experience as sacred or Divine? And what is my relationship to it? With Contemplation, we develop a different kind of interiority, one that goes simultaneously deeper into the depths of our being and wider, expanding toward the outer, to see how we are embedded in the

Cosmos, in relationship to it, to all other beings, and to whatever we understand as that which is greater than us, or ultimately real. It is one ear turned inwards and one turn out.

Ed Bastian, founder of the Spiritual Paths Foundation and creator of Interspiritual Meditation, describes Contemplation as a reflective process of "Going deeply within our own being, bringing us into the presence of an essential reality." It is a state of consciousness that "Lies at the border of deep conceptual thinking, sudden inspiration, and pure meditational tranquility."

Contemplation is the fulcrum or turning point from our first five words toward our second five. We move from personal cultivation to a relational way of being, from *being* to *doing*. In Contemplation, we enter what Martin Buber called the "I-Thou," or the dialogic relationship between ourselves and the Divine *as we experience it*.

Contemplation becomes the throughline of our entire practice. Through Contemplation, we deepen our practices of Attention, Acceptance, Authenticity, Benevolence, and Balance, and it is *through* Contemplation that we bring those qualities into action in the world in the remaining words.

Without a conscious turning of the mind and heart away from the mundane, even for a few minutes a day, we remain mired in our mundane lives, small selves, and petty concerns. In other words, without a dedication to some practice of Contemplation, we cannot truly see our spiritual path, call ourselves "spiritual," or integrate our spiritual life into action in the world.

WHY IS CONTEMPLATION IMPORTANT?

> *God is not a goal to be achieved. God is a presence to*
> *be recognized. ... It starts with the contemplation and*
> *consciousness of the Mystery, which is the only reason, the*
> *only possibility of ever developing a truly spiritual life.*

SR. JOAN CHITTISTER

In every tradition, contemplative practice forms the basis of a relationship to the Divine, whatever form that might take. All the mystics of every tradition have spent their lives in deep contemplation, seeking a connection with the Divine that can only be found through silence, solitude, meditation, prayer, devotion, or study. From their contemplation, the great religious traditions were born.

Etymologically, contemplation comes from roots that mean "the act of looking or gazing attentively." In Latin, *con-* means "with," and *templum* refers to a temple, which was a space "cut out" or removed from the everyday reality, consecrated for worship, or "occupied by Divine presence." Contemplation then becomes action, which is separated from mundane life specifically because its focus is an attentive gaze to the bigger picture or the Divine. We intentionally enter "the temple" to spend time with the Divine.

To keep from being overwhelmed by the demands of the world and our own minds, we need silence, space to shut out the world, come back to ourselves and listen. That's really what Contemplation is: a time and space to listen to what it real, true and necessary for ourselves. The Benedictines call it the cloister, a protected, private space, or the cell.

Of course, the doctrines of each tradition define contemplation differently. Each tradition also has different contemplative practices.

There are, however, commonalities. Dr. Louis Komjathy, an expert in Comparative Contemplative Studies, characterizes contemplation across traditions as having or evoking six qualities: attentiveness, awareness, interiority, presence, silence, transformation, and a deepened sense of meaning and purpose.

Many of these qualities are already familiar to us from our practice of the previous five words. But there is a broader, more inclusive way of thinking about the purpose and practice of contemplation. In the classic *New Seeds of Contemplation*, Christian monk and mystic Thomas Merton describes Contemplation this way:

> Contemplation is the highest expression of man's intellectual and spiritual life. It is that life itself, fully awake, fully active, fully aware that it is alive. It is a spiritual wonder. It is spontaneous awe at the sacredness of life, of being. It is gratitude for life, for awareness, and for being. It is a vivid realization of the fact that life and being in us proceed from an invisible, transcendent and infinitely abundant Source. Contemplation, above all, is an awareness of the reality of that Source.

In other words, Contemplation is how we begin to develop an awareness of that which is both integral to and greater than ourselves, which we might call True Self, Spirit, Source, Mystery, Ultimate Reality, the Divine, God, the Cosmos, the Dao, Buddha-mind, Brahman—or no name at all. In his book *Handbook for Jewish Meditation Practices*, Rabbi David Cooper says, "Human consciousness seeks to know the truth of its own existence, its source, and its reason for being."

By turning our attention toward experiencing and understanding that which surrounds us and of which we are indivisible, we begin to discover our place in the greater scheme of things and, for some, a personal relationship with whatever we might experience as the Divine. In every tradition, Contemplation is about cultivating a relationship with whatever it is that we call "Divinity," both within and without.

Bede Griffiths, a Catholic and Hindu monk, described it this way: "We see our life for a moment in its true perspective in relation to eternity. We are freed from the flux of time and see something of the eternal order which underlies it. We are no longer isolated individuals in conflict with our surroundings; we are parts of a whole, elements in a universal harmony."

The act of contemplation comes from a deep longing, a desire to know and be united with the True Self, Truth, the bigger picture, or the Divine, that is at the heart of a spiritual life. In fact, one cannot truly call oneself "spiritual" without that desire on some level. Rumi points to it in his poem, "Love Dogs," when he tells the story of a man calling for Allah all night long until his lips bled, disappointed not to receive an answer, only to learn that his longing itself was the response. In his book, *God in Search of Man*, Rabbi Abraham Joshua Heschel also explains the desire for God as God's desire for us. The Divine wants to know us as much as we want to know the Divine. The Biblical psalmist cries, "My soul longs for you, O God. My soul thirsts for God, for the living God" (Psalm 42:1-2), and Christian mystic Meister Eckhart believed that the inherent desire of all beings to know God was the ordering principle of the universe itself!

Daoists, Buddhists, and Hindus also stress the desire to know or attain the Dao, Buddha-nature, or *Brahman* as the ultimate motivation of spiritual life, and their techniques of meditation are contemplative practices for precisely that purpose. Classical yoga, in its true form, is a contemplative practice that means "union." The purpose of yoga is *samadhi* or absorption in the Divine.

Islamic contemplation is synonymous with "remembrance"— remembering and experiencing the presence of the Almighty through contemplation of both the created and the Creator. In fact, in the Qur'an, it is stated that the contemplation of Allah's creation is one of the greatest forms of worship. Even indigenous traditions use contemplation in some form—often through music, dance, ceremony, and deep meditation or trance—to experience and merge with the spiritual world.

What is experienced in this union with or knowledge of the Divine? Though categorically unexplainable, thousands of pages have been devoted to articulating the experience of the Divine, and those words form the very basis of all spiritual traditions. If we look at what they all have in common, we discover similar language: awe, wonder, love, bliss, peace, union, oneness, mystery, emptiness, and darkness.

In other words, we can't really explain it, but through Contemplation, we can directly experience it. When we do, that's what is often called "Awakening" or "Enlightenment." Mechtild of Magdeburg, an early Christian mystic, explains, "The day of my spiritual awakening was the day I saw—and knew I saw—all things in God and God in all things." In other words, Mechtild "awakened" to the reality of something bigger than herself that is everywhere.

It might sound like Contemplation is reserved for prophets, saints, sages, monks, and mystics, spending long hours in their cells, caves, mountaintop hermitages, or wandering the desert, but it's not. It's for everyone. It's something we can do every day, even if we are sitting in traffic.

It's really just a shift of focus and the cultivation of an awareness of something bigger than ourselves. Even if we don't have the longing for union with the Divine or Enlightenment, we can use Contemplation as a practice for learning to be present, be open, be receptive, to see ourselves, others, and the world as it is, without concept, in its fullness and mystery, and to deepen our relationship to it.

With time, a contemplative practice transforms us and makes it possible to be surrounded by the chaos and suffering of life and remain centered, calm, and joyful. Even psychologists and physicians agree that awareness of something beyond ourselves is necessary for mental health, and calming the mind and body relieves stress that causes disease.

Moreover, in difficult times, we are called to act in the world, and these days, it's almost unavoidable. However, that action must come from a contemplative place, from an understanding of what is real, and a place of authentic relationship to that. Otherwise, it is likely to be ineffective at best or deeply destructive at worst. It is only through Contemplation that action becomes authentic. In other words, true action is contemplative and authentic contemplation acts.

HOW TO BRING CONTEMPLATION INTO YOUR LIFE

God is not found in the soul by adding
anything but by a process of subtraction
MEISTER ECKHART

In modern English usage, we take contemplation to mean thinking about something. But in a spiritual context, Contemplation is not a "thinking" process; it's not intellectual or discursive. You can't figure it out. It's not factual. It's not using our imagination. It's experiential. It's more of a sensing or intuition. In Contemplation, we go past knowing facts or concepts to a deeper "knowing" that often cannot be articulated in words. We allow ourselves to "see without eyes, hear without ears."

In Hebrew, the word is *Hitbodedut,* or inward retreat, through which we enter what the 14th century anonymous Christian mystic called "The Cloud of Unknowing," 13th century Kabbalist Azriel of Gerona termed "nothingness of thought" or Zen masters refer to as "Empty Mind." The Daode Jing, verse 16 describes the process perfectly:

> Empty yourself of everything.
> Let the mind become still.
> The ten thousand things rise and fall while the
>   self watches their return.
> They grow and flourish and then return to the source.
> Returning to the source is stillness, which is the way
>   of nature.

Mystics from all traditions have described one of the fruits of contemplation as the experience of returning to Source, union with the Divine, or merging with Buddha-Mind or the Dao. But the way to experience that union is through the transcendence of self. It's a subtractive process or what theologian Matthew Fox calls the *Via Negativa,* or the Kabbalists call *Be-Bittul,* releasing the self.

In Contemplation, we move from the egoic self to the trans-egoic; we release the "I" of Identity to see the "I" in everything or everything in the "I." In other words, we let go of "self" with a small *s* to experience "Self" with a capital *S,* the very movement we discussed in Authenticity only at a higher octave. It is both an emptying out and being emptied of thoughts, beliefs, stories, concepts, and images of ourselves and the world around us so we can truly see and know what is. Releasing our long-cherished beliefs and illusions can be challenging for many. But if we don't try, we will never begin to experience what is really *real*.

Some have described it as a sinking or descending from the head into the heart. Again, Merton explains, "We do not detach ourselves from things in order to attach ourselves to God, but rather we become detached from ourselves in order to see and use all things in and for God." This is the function and purpose of all Contemplation.

THERE'S NOTHING TO DO

Though there are countless techniques for Contemplation, there is really nothing to "do" in Contemplation. In fact, it's the opposite; it's a not-doing. It's a surrender. Letting go. You cannot *not* think by thinking about not thinking. And yet, it has intention and discipline.

This isn't free wandering of the mind to think about anything it wants but a focused *release* of discursive, rambling thinking. As Zen Roshi John Daido Loori says, "Just sitting does not involve reaching some understanding. It is the subtle activity of allowing all things to be completely at rest just as they are, not poking one's head into the workings of the world."

THERE'S NO PLACE TO GO

At the same time, Contemplation is not something we achieve. It's not a fixed state but an ongoing process, a constant emptying out of concepts, beliefs, language, and images until nothing remains but clear awareness.

Merton warns that "The success of your meditation will not be measured by the brilliant ideas you get or the great resolutions you make or the feelings and emotions that are produced in your exterior senses. You have only really meditated well when you have come, to some extent, to realize God. Yet even that is not quite the thing."

THERE'S NOTHING TO GET

Nor is Contemplation something that gives us magical powers of healing, prophecy, or revelation, though sometimes, we may "know" things that aren't available to us through our normal sensory or intellectual perception. Contemplation, as the action of being open and receptive, sets the stage for some form of experiencing or knowing that is trans-temporal and trans-egoic.

All traditions have some kind of doctrinal description of the Divine and the possible effect of contemplation on the practitioner. For example, you might "see" Jesus, some type of deity, or vast, interconnected oneness or emptiness. But we cannot go into Contemplation with a fixed idea of what we will find when we get there. Just as you don't start a new relationship with preconceived notions of your partner, you must approach Contemplation with openness, curiosity, and a willingness to discover and learn.

In truth, we cannot enter Contemplation with expectations of any kind, especially that we will experience that bliss of union or enlightenment. If we do, we will be sorely disappointed. That may or may not happen. It's not something we can "make happen." We cannot force knowledge. Instead, we come to Contemplation without expectation and view it simply as time spent quietly with ourselves and the Divine, and we just see what happens.

BEGINNING A
CONTEMPLATIVE PRACTICE

There are many ways to approach a contemplative practice: prayer, meditation, sacred reading, chanting, visualization, music, movement, devotional practices, art, and time in nature. In the next section, we will take a walk-through of how to practice focused contemplation through an exploration of some techniques drawn from the great traditions.

Regardless of the technique involved, Contemplation is simply the release of the discursive mind to focus on being in receptive silence with God/True Self/The Divine. Essentially, it is being quiet, letting your mind empty, and being open to what arises. It's that deeper form of Awareness we spoke about in Attention. However, what all forms of Contemplation have in common is a dedicated practice. Contemplation is something we need to do regularly and consistently for it to have any effect.

PREPARATION

Preparation is important. In the beginning, it's very hard to just "contemplate." You must set the stage for it; you must enter the temple. In some ways, we have been preparing for this since we began our journey with the Ten Words. We have learned to pay attention to our thoughts, feelings, and actions, and maybe we even learned to be in open awareness, but now we must release all of that to experience something beyond ourselves.

To begin, choose a time and a place to be alone, without the phone or other distractions. It might be someplace in your home, in nature, or in a sacred building like a church, temple, meditation hall, or mosque. It might be for a few minutes early in the morning or before you go to bed. It might be one day a week or every day. Consider this time and place a "sacred space" and "time-out-of-time." If you keep returning to that place and time, your mind and body will become accustomed to it and be entrained to "Contemplation Time."

Choose a technique that appeals to you from those listed below or others you prefer or discover. Pick one to start and be consistent with it. Give it a few weeks. Don't bounce around from one technique to the other. The fruits of contemplation don't come right away. It takes time for the mind and body to entrain. The more you do it, the more likely you are to experience some of the true effects (though remember that we aren't after anything specific). If, after a time, you want to explore another form of contemplation or add to your first one, feel free, but again, give it a few weeks of practice before you go to something else.

Set a timer and be in contemplation for ten to twenty minutes, more if you choose. You may find that at the beginning, it's hard to be still and quiet for even a few minutes. That's normal. We aren't used to being still and quiet and alone. Just keep doing it, and you will become more accustomed to it. Generally, ten to thirty minutes is fine, but like everything else, make it consistent. Don't stop until the time you've set is up. When your time is up, slowly re-enter the world.

One way to help make contemplation a regular practice and to keep going through the challenging parts is to consider it a special time and place, just for you and the Divine to be alone, away from the hustle and bustle, schedule, and obligations of daily life. A regular date with God, the Cosmos, or your true inner self. Sometimes, that date might be challenging; other times, it's peaceful and easy. Be patient. Let go of expectations and just keep coming back. That's how you build a relationship: one date at a time.

THE TECHNIQUES

There are many techniques for contemplation from all spiritual traditions. Some are simple, and some are very complex and esoteric. Visualization practices, such as those from the more mystical teachings or indigenous shamanistic traditions, can be very involved and specific. In many cases, they require deep immersion into the theology of a given tradition or initiation and can be extremely powerful for altering consciousness. We do not offer those techniques here. If you are interested in exploring those, do so with an experienced teacher.

The techniques presented here are common to all traditions, even though their forms might vary. I have selected a few practices that are interspiritual at their core, do not require any specific theological knowledge, and are easy to learn and practice. That does not mean they aren't powerful; done consistently, they can change your life. However, regardless of the technique used, they all have the same purpose: to release the discursive mind and to be open and receptive to the Divine, the True Self, or spiritual knowledge.

Meditation

Meditation is often synonymous with contemplation, but not all meditation is contemplative. These days, we often see meditation as a tool for psychological health, but in this case, we aren't talking about the popular guided visualizations/meditations used to calm our nervous systems, the forms of meditation in which we watch and label our thoughts, or rumination about negative behaviors. Contemplative meditation is different; we are letting go of our "stuff" to experience something else. As it is said in the Psalms, "Be still and know that I am God."

Every tradition has some form of contemplative meditation. Contemplative meditation might focus on a specific word, mantra, breath, object, visualization, sound, or image at the beginning to calm our minds, such as chanting *Om* or paying attention to the in and out of our breath, gazing at a candle flame or an icon, or holding an image in our minds. But in most, once we have reached a certain point, contemplative meditation asks us to let go of that focus and sit in silence and stillness until we become absorbed. In the Hasidic tradition, the absorption of God experienced in meditation is called *Devekut.* In Zen, it is Empty Mind.

Hindu *Dhyana,* Zen *Shikan Taza* or Empty Sitting meditation, Krishnamurti's techniqueless meditation, and Daoist *Zuowong* meditation are just a few of these techniques. They are classified as "introverted" meditation, as they focus on the inward experience by completely shutting out the outside world. These meditations also don't begin with any image or word. They just go right to the empty mind by sitting still, releasing thoughts, and allowing the mind to relax its need to analyze, explain, judge, name, or understand.

Zen Teacher Taizan Maezumi tells us why: "As long as we remain within the confines of the thinking mind, we can't experience the state of non-thinking. If we can't experience non-thinking, we will not understand what our life truly is. Please realize this for yourself! Just sit." There are many resources and classes for learning this type of meditation online and in print. Explore any and all that call to you.

Islamic Meditation includes the Sufi practices of *Murqabah,* but the more traditional *Tafakkur* is a well-developed system of contemplative practice that is different from other forms of meditation in that the focus is more outward. Designed to bring the practitioner's attention to the Oneness of God, *Tafakkur* focuses on understanding our place in the wider universe through the appreciation of Allah's creation. By turning one's attention to nature, art, or other forms of creation with an open, receptive mind, the practitioner experiences the Divine Creator in all things.

For example, we could look at our hands and notice their strength, delicacy, and usefulness. How amazing is it that we have hands? Or the sun. We feel its warmth, power, and light, without which we would cease to exist. We could listen to music and allow ourselves to be transported by it. Again, we aren't looking at things discursively or to "understand," but to allow ourselves to come with an open, quiet, empty mind and, in that space, discover something about the nature of ourselves and/or the Divine.

There is also a practice of art as meditation. The creative process is not dissimilar to any other form of meditation. To create art, we must empty ourselves to allow the images and forms to come through us unobstructed. When making art, we are also in a state of internal quiet, listening only for that impulse that leads to the next line, the next stroke of the brush, or the next note.

In Zen, for example, the practices of ink brush painting or flower arranging are forms of meditation. In medieval Christianity, the painting of icons, frescos, and illuminated manuscripts were also high forms of contemplation by monks. In all cases, art as meditation is less about the creation of an object of art for sale or show but about the process of creating, or the contemplative state of mind of the artist. My own teacher used to assign long art practices to students as a very concentrated form of meditation.

Regardless of the form of meditation, focused or contentless, inward or outward, from any tradition, the point is to release what you think you know about yourself, the world, or the Divine to experience it fully and truly. It is, as Ed Bastian explains, "An activity that connects us to an aspect of human consciousness that has the capacity to become tranquil, one-pointed, non-conceptual and unified with the Ultimate Reality."

Prayer

In the Christian, Jewish, and Islamic traditions, contemplation most often takes the form of prayer. Whether through Quaker Silent Prayer, Jewish *Amidah*, the Early Christian Hesychastic prayer, or Sufi *Dhikr/Zikr*, contemplative prayer is a cornerstone of each tradition.

Unlike prayer as a form of praise, supplication, confession, or thanksgiving, contemplative prayer is the opportunity to be alone with the Divine, as if with a dear friend or lover, with no agenda. Father Thomas Keating defines this kind of prayer as "A conversation with God." When we spend time with one another in intimate conversation, we open ourselves up with honesty and vulnerability and listen attentively to each other. That's all that contemplative prayer is—an opportunity to share intimate time with your True Self, Higher Self, or the Divine.

Keating and fellow forward-thinking Catholic monks created a form of contemplative prayer that makes that conversation with God easier. It's called Centering Prayer and derives from the ancient Christian Hesychastic practices in which the practitioner was instructed to empty the mind of any thoughts, passions, ideas, emotions, or images to make space for the "Voice of God."

According to Centering Prayer teacher Cynthia Bourgeault, the process begins with the "intention to consent to the presence and action of God within." Again, intention must precede attention. Then, choose a sacred word that you can hold in your mind, one or two syllables that remind you of the Divinity of your understanding, such as Jesus, Mary, Allah, Adonai, or Buddha, or a state, such as peace, joy, or love. Sit still in a comfortable position in silence for ten to twenty minutes, allowing thoughts and emotions to dissipate or drain out, returning to your sacred word in your mind whenever distractions occur. The idea is to simply allow thoughts and concerns to be released so that the inner voice, or the voice of God, can be heard.

Centering Prayer is almost identical to a technique used by Hasidic mystics called *gerushin*, or repetition, and is not dissimilar to contemplative meditation. It is applicable to any tradition or none, as the sacred word you choose can be anything that speaks to you and reminds you to turn your attention to that which is both within and beyond. Even for those who cringe at the word "prayer," Centering Prayer is a useful contemplative practice. It is simply time spent in silence, without thinking, allowing the Divine or your Inner Self to talk.

Contemplative Reading

Lectio Divina, a Latin term that means contemplative reading of sacred text, is another form of contemplation that comes from the Christian tradition but is applicable to any tradition or none. In *Lectio Divina*, we allow the text to "speak" to us, not as a critical reading exercise or to gain information, but as a kind of subtle spiritual direction or prompt for our contemplation.

Traditionally, *Lectio* meant reading the Bible, but we can use any kind of sacred text, poetry, or even some secular texts. To begin, choose a passage to read. Sit quietly and read slowly, not for information or to get through it, but to allow the words to speak to you and seep in beneath the surface of the discursive mind. If something calls to you, stop, put the book down, sit quietly, and let yourself absorb it. Don't try to analyze it or engage your critical mind. Just allow whatever arises to arise. What is it trying to say about a spiritual life? What does it mean to you? How does it call to your spiritual self? *Lectio* is a process, a dialogue between you and the words on the page. It's meant to prod insight.

You can reread the passage or carry on, but remember, this isn't about studying a text for intellectual understanding; this is about listening to what is being offered to you as if listening to a friend. How does it make you feel? What "knowing" is there?

Lectio Divina can also take other forms besides that of reading. We can contemplate art, especially sacred art, nature, music, or even our own bodies, similar to Islamic *Tafakkur*. Anything can be the source of spiritual "knowledge" if we approach it that way, if we listen or gaze attentively with openness and curiosity, not to understand intellectually, but with an eye and ear tuned to what is beyond the intellect.

Nature Contemplation

All indigenous and mystical traditions have a deep contemplative relationship with the natural world. Observing clouds, mountains, water, plants, and animals led mystics and sages to a profound understanding and relationship to the Divine. Of course, many prophets and teachers spent large amounts of time in the wilderness of the mountains or desert, allowing them to contemplate in silence and solitude. As a result, all great spiritual texts refer to nature and the natural world as reflections of the Divine. Even Thoreau, the American Transcendentalist, once wrote, "Nature is so full of genius, full of divinity, so that not a snowflake escapes its fashioning hand."

The Japanese practice of Forest Bathing has become popular, and though considered a health and wellness practice in Japan, it is an easy way to use nature as a contemplative practice. It involves spending time in nature with the intention of listening to, observing, and experiencing the plants, trees, sounds, and feelings or "sensing" that arise. Simply go into a forest, park, beach, desert, riverside, or anywhere surrounded by nature, or, if you can't, just watch a sunset, gaze at clouds, or even spend time with your houseplants. Empty your mind of the mundane, be quiet, and turn your attention receptively to the environment itself. You might sit or walk, but keep your attention turned toward nature; don't let it wander off to work or your weekend plans. Remember, this is not an exercise to study nature. We aren't looking for what we can learn through our discursive mind, but we are attentive to what arises.

Even a single flower can be a form of nature meditation. As Zen master Shunryu Suzuki once said, "Someone was sitting in front of a sunflower, watching the sunflower, a cup of sun, and so I tried it too. It was wonderful; I felt the whole universe in the sunflower. Sunflower meditation!"

Devotional Contemplation

Though it may seem like some devotional practices are the opposite of still and quiet, they are another gateway into Contemplation that brings our attention squarely to something larger than ourselves. Hindu *puja* and *kirtan*, the ecstatic praise songs of Hasidic Judaism, rousing Christian hymns and Gospel songs, Sufi *Dhikr* or *Sama*, altar practices from a wide range of traditions, worship services, indigenous rituals and ceremonies, and many other traditional forms of devotion can inspire us to contemplate our relationship to that which is greater than ourselves.

While many of these practices are specific to a particular tradition or theological understanding, altars are a simple, ecumenical way to begin a devotional contemplative practice and serve as both a container and a focus for contemplation—like a temple. Today, many people have a home altar of some kind. It might just be a shelf or a tabletop where we place meaningful objects and photographs of people we love. It may be more formal, with statues or icons of deities or spiritual teachers, or very simple: a candle and perhaps an incense holder. Some have spaces in nature, perhaps a favorite tree or rock that is visited regularly. Others use altars in public spaces, like churches or temples. A woman I know makes a mini-altar from found natural objects every day on her morning walk.

Make an altar for yourself with objects, images, or other items that remind you of your understanding of the Divine. To engage your altar, you might simply light a candle or burn some incense. You might have a prayer or poem that you recite, a chant, or a meaningful song. You may offer something else: a flower, a piece of fruit, a cup of tea, a written note, or anything symbolic of your willingness to let go, be present with your True Self or the Divine of your understanding, and be open to what you might learn.

Whatever you choose to do at your altar, spend time with it, let it be part of your "Conversation with the Divine," and allow yourself to sit in still silence for a few minutes. You can also use an altar practice as a preliminary activity to aid you in entering a contemplative state.

CONTEMPLATIVE SOUND AND MOVEMENT

As we know, the mind and body are not separate, and all traditions use movement, sound, singing, or chanting to induce a contemplative state. While not Contemplation itself, these practices are adjuncts or aids to calm the mind and focus it so that Contemplation becomes possible. You might want to use one of these techniques to help you enter Contemplation.

Chanting

Chanting is used in all traditions to bring the mind and body into coherence to begin silent contemplation. Chants tend to have repetitive, simple melodies and text, so the mind is occupied, but there is no need to use the mind to remember, allowing it to empty. Our ancestors knew instinctively what neuroscience has proven: certain tones and rhythms can induce a trance-like state, changing the brain waves to expand our consciousness. Contemplation is all about expanding our sense of self from the small "s" to the capital "S."

When we chant, contemplation of the words sung or chanted can bring our attention to the Divine, similar to the use of text in *Lectio Divina.* The Gregorian chants of medieval Christianity, chanted recitation of Buddhist sutras, Hindu mantras, the recitation of the 99 names of God in the Islamic tradition, Kabbalistic *Haggah,* or the 72 Names of God, Hasidic *nigunnim,* or melodic syllables, and many indigenous songs and chants, are a few examples of contemplative chanting. There are many simple chants from all traditions, but you could also make one up for yourself. Simply choose a phrase that reminds you of the Divine of your understanding, or choose one to four simple syllables to repeat aloud in a simple melody.

Musical instruments

Repetitive and simple musical instruments—bowls, bells, gongs, flutes, drums—are also used to induce a trance or contemplative state, and every tradition uses some form of musical practice as a contemplative aid. Whether playing them or listening to them, the discursive mind relaxes, and we are open to hearing and experiencing something beyond ourselves. Try listening to or playing a simple instrument at the beginning of your contemplation practice. Even striking a small prayer bowl or bell will bring your mind into focus.

Movement

Many traditions use repetitive, simple movement to induce a contemplative state. Again, while not always actual Contemplation itself, contemplative movement can help bring the practitioner into a physical and mental state in which Contemplation can happen. The postures of Islamic *salat*, the prostrations of Buddhists, Catholic Rosary or Buddhist/Hindu *mala* prayer beads, Daoist circle walking, Sufi whirling, Yogic *asana* and *pranayama* (breathwork), Jewish *daven*, and the many forms of indigenous dance are good examples that can not only induce a trance-like state but also can precede a period of silence and stillness in which Contemplation can begin.

If movement helps you focus and release your thoughts, explore simple yoga, t'ai chi, breathing practices, or prostrations, or try something simple like prayer beads.

CONTEMPLATION OFF THE CUSHION

Initially, we must cultivate our inner stillness and silence very intentionally through dedicated practice. However, with consistent effort, we can maintain that still, quiet, open, receptive awareness throughout our day, in most situations, resulting in a much more easeful life.

Buddhist monk and teacher Thich Nhat Hahn was famous for his sayings that urged people to use everyday actions as an opportunity to be present. We can do the same with Contemplation: can you wash the dishes contemplatively? Can you make dinner contemplatively?

Call that client contemplatively? Can you deal with your kids or spouse from a contemplative place?

When we bring our Contemplation "off the cushion," we find that even amid chaos and pain, we can maintain a sense of balance, equilibrium, and centeredness that can only come from familiarity with that still point within. And, when we practice Contemplation in every moment of our day, we discover something even deeper: a profound, unchanging joy, wonder, and awe, an ability to sit with and through pain, inner strength that comes from self-knowing, and an unshakeable trust in the Divine, Source, or Dao. Some call that faith.

Our ability to remain open, calm, and centered throughout the activities of our days also rubs off on others. Many times, I have been in the presence of someone whose contemplative approach and simple, peaceful, and warm demeanor were the catalyst for conflict resolution within and between people. Somehow, without saying anything overtly, everyone calmed down and dealt with each other from a deeply compassionate place. The presence of the contemplative person was the teaching itself, and the fruits of their practice affected others.

A CONTEMPLATIVE IN THE WORLD

In the past, the contemplative life was seen as distinct from or opposite to action in the world. Monks and nuns in all traditions, the paragons of contemplatives, lived separated from the mundane world and focused solely on their spiritual cultivation. But that's a misleading concept: many deeply contemplative spiritual leaders and prophets in every tradition took their contemplation to the streets. Moses, Jesus, The Prophet Mohammed (PBUH), Buddha, Gandhi, Mother Teresa, Rev. Dr. Martin Luther King, Jr., and others used the fruits of their contemplation in action. They contemplated deeply, and from their contemplations, they were moved to action whether to teach, heal, protest, or care for the earth and her inhabitants.

In his autobiography, *The Seven Story Mountain*, Catholic monk and activist Thomas Merton says we are all called to contemplation and that the results of our contemplative practice are to be shared with others. Merton writes,

> Whether you teach or live in the cloister or nurse the sick, whether you are in religion or out of it, married or single, no matter who you are or what you are, you are called to the summit of perfection: you are called to a deep interior life perhaps even to mystical prayer, and to pass the fruits of your contemplation on to others.

While contemplative practice can bring us to states of joy, bliss, and peace, it can also bring us into direct contact with the suffering in the world, both our own and others. It stirs our compassion and our desire to help relieve that suffering. Contemplative practice also leads us to recognize our interdependence, our deep connection to others and the world around us, and how we can serve one another from a genuine place of benevolence and love. In Jewish teachings, this is called *Tikkun Olam*, or perfecting the world through raising our consciousness to the deep interconnectedness of all beings and serving that interconnectedness through compassion and justice.

These days, the imperative to bring the fruits of our contemplation into the world is strong. To live from your spiritual center requires engagement in the world in some way. We can no longer be contemplatives sitting on our mountaintop, focused only on our self-cultivation to the exclusion of others.

How that action appears in the world will differ for each of us. It might mean that through our contemplative practice, we are moved to do something publicly, to protest or work actively for change on a socio-political level, or it might mean that we bring our awareness and compassion to others more privately through our personal relationships, creative work, or care of the people, land, plants, and animals we tend.

The important thing is that we do not separate our contemplation from action. They are interrelated; one feeds the other and vice versa. Our contemplative practice might move us to action in the world, and then the action itself becomes a contemplative practice; we approach it with openness, curiosity, and attention. What can we learn from it? How does it bring us closer to understanding ourselves, others, the world around us, and the Divine?

PRACTICE, PRACTICE, PRACTICE

As stated earlier, Contemplation is something you must do regularly to reap the benefits, and the results of a contemplative life are immeasurable. It might be hard at first, and when you truly begin to explore it, you might experience things that make you question your beliefs or illusions, but that's the point: to get you to see Reality as it is. Just begin your contemplative practice, knowing that it might change over time. Show up to it with intention. Soon, it will become like your best friend, something or someone you don't want to be without.

In truth, if you do nothing else, practice Contemplation. You could never read another spiritual book or learn other practices and still reach tremendous spiritual insight, self-realization, or just be a better person if you simply cultivate a contemplative practice. Your

Contemplation is your best teacher; without it, your journey will be incomplete.

All the spiritual traditions agree. Contemplation is *the* central practice of most Eastern traditions: "Just sit." The early Christian Desert Fathers and Mothers used to say, "Go to your cell. It will teach you everything." And the Talmud teaches: "All my life, I have lived among wise teachers, yet I found nothing better for oneself than silence. Rather than study, practice is the main teacher" (Pirke Avot 1:17).

> *The ultimate value of life depends upon awareness and the*
> *power of contemplation rather than upon mere survival.*
>
> ARISTOTLE

REFLECTION QUESTIONS

1. What does Contemplation mean to me?

2. Why is Contemplation important to me?

3. How do I practice Contemplation? What contemplative practice(s) do I want to explore?

4. What prevents me from Contemplation?

5. What arises in my contemplation? What do I experience?

6. How can I deepen those experiences through a more concentrated contemplative practice?

7. In what ways do I experience the Divine?

8. When I act in the world, do my actions come from a contemplative place?

9. Can I be more contemplative in my daily life?

SUGGESTED PRACTICES

Set aside a specific time/day for Contemplation. It can be daily or weekly, but make it consistent. Choose a space that is comfortable and free from distraction. Set a timer for ten to twenty minutes. Choose one technique to focus on for the month—prayer, meditation, nature contemplation, devotion, or *Lectio Divina*—and, if you want, a preliminary technique such as chanting, music, or movement to help you enter a contemplative state. Allow yourself to be still and quiet.

1. Explore Centering Prayer or the Quaker form of Silent Prayer.

2. Explore Contemplative Meditation from any tradition. Or an art meditation practice.

3. Find a text you would like to read contemplatively for the month, such as *Lectio Divina*. If you prefer, explore sacred art or music and use that as a form of *Lectio Divina*.

4. Get out in nature. Allow your mind to empty and simply be present with the natural world.

5. Build an altar and engage it regularly.

6. Try chanting, music, or a movement practice to help you enter a contemplative state.

7. Explore how your contemplative practice might move you to action and how your daily actions can be approached contemplatively.

7

Creativity

The creative process, like a spiritual journey, is
intuitive, non-linear, and experiential. It points us
toward our essential nature, which is a reflection
of the boundless creativity of the universe.

JOHN DAIDO LOORI

The Cosmos is creative, constantly birthing the new—new galaxies, stars, beings, and events. In all traditions, this creative force is the essence of the Divine, whether as a Creator God or as that ineffable source that generates or gives birth to all form (and is all form). That includes us. We are, by definition, creators. Every moment of our lives is our creation.

Embracing Creativity is an essential part of our spiritual path. As we align with the creative energies of the Divine, we begin to see ourselves as co-creators who can bring into existence that which did not exist before. Matthew Fox, theologian and proponent of Creation Spirituality, explains, "Creativity is where the divine and the human meet."

Creativity doesn't just mean painting, dancing, or writing. While the creative process is a profound form of alignment with the Creator,

Creativity really refers to every action in our lives that involves the imagination, or the transformation of what is to *what might be possible*. Cooking a meal, tending a garden, building a business, raising children, or testing a scientific theory are all creative acts that bring into being that which didn't exist until we created it. Like the Divine, we are bringing the world into existence moment by moment through our creative imagination. But Creativity doesn't stop there; it's in every word, thought, and deed of our daily lives. Every moment is a creative one.

Creativity often comes out of Contemplation. When we are still and quiet, we are often inspired by an idea that arises. Or, if we are in contemplation of nature or art, we become aware of the creative energy of the Divine at work in everything, everywhere, and that inspires us. It is said that beauty is a sign of the good. Our recognition of the beauty that surrounds us is brings us closer to the Divine. That's another side of Creativity: the appreciation of the creative work of others, even God.

WHY IS CREATIVITY IMPORTANT?

God is our Creator. God made us in his likeness and his
image. Therefore, we are creators. He gave us a garden to toil
and cultivate. We became co-creators through our responsible
acts, whether in bringing forth children or producing food,
furniture, or clothing. The joy of creativeness should be ours.
DOROTHY DAY

From nothingness comes somethingness. That is the basis of all creation stories ever told whether in the Bible or the Daode Jing, the Vedas, or the Qu'ran. There was nothing, and then God, the Dao, or whatever each tradition calls the Divine, "birthed" all things into existence. The Divine created, generated, emanated, or manifested what we experience. And, most importantly, it's still happening. Always.

Christian mystic Meister Eckhart said very simply, "What does God do all day? God gives birth. From all eternity, God lies on a maternity bed giving birth." He explains further: "Now God creates all things but does not stop creating. God forever creates and forever begins to create, and creatures are always being created and in the process of beginning to be created."

In the Hebrew Bible, the very first words written are *Beresheit bara Elohim*, "In the beginning, God created." It is the very foundation of existence. The names of God in the Hebrew Bible describe the creative processes of becoming and existence. The word for God's creativity is *Dabhar*, often translated as "the word." It was God's word, or his creative imagination, that created the world. Words create reality, and in Genesis, God gives Adam the ability to name—or to give word to—all the beings of the earth. In naming them, Adam is also creating their reality.

In the Hindu Vedas, the creation of the universe is explained as a force of energy from a Supreme Being, or, in another version, a lotus flower grew from Lord Vishnu's navel with Brahma sitting on it. Brahma separated the flower into three parts—the heavens, the earth, and the sky. Out of loneliness, Brahma split himself into two to create a male and a female. From this male and female, all beings were created. Many indigenous traditions have similar creation myths.

Though there are no creator deities in the non-dual traditions of Vedantic Hinduism, Daoism, and Buddhism, there are still emergence or creation stories. In Daoism, the Dao is seen as a non-dual chaos or undifferentiated oneness *without* intention from which all things emerge, emanate, arise, or are generated. Yin and yang, the mascu-line/feminine or creative/receptive forces, emerged from the Dao. From their interaction, "the ten thousand things" arise and are con-tinually in processes of change and transformation. Buddhists believe the beginning of this world and life is inconceivable since they have neither beginning nor end. Therefore, Buddhists and Daoists believe that the world was not created once upon a time but is created mil-lions of times every second and will continue to do so by itself.

This last belief aligns with modern science. Cosmologists now have a theory called *Cosmogenesis*, which proposes that the Cosmos itself is always in the process of creation and transformation. In other words, the Cosmos itself is in a process of continuous creation. In his book, *The Great Work*, Ecologist Thomas Berry describes it this way: "We now live not so much in a *cosmos* as in a *cosmogenesis*; that is, a universe ever coming into being through an irreversible sequence of transfor-mations moving, in the larger arc of its development, from a lesser to a great order of complexity and from a lesser to great consciousness."

This suggests that the world wasn't simply created in a final form a few thousand years ago, as some sacred texts would assert, but is con-stantly evolving. Simple observation will tell us that the world is noth-ing like what it was when the Bible, the Qu'ran, or many other creation scriptures were written. It has changed! In many cases, very dramati-cally. Moreover, science tells us that world is a very different place now compared to when we *homo sapiens*, a new species, first appeared. All of this is to say that science and religion agree that creativity is inher-ent in the Cosmos; everything in the Cosmos is in a state of constant creation and transformation from minute to minute. And so are we.

Our "always in the process of beginning to be created" is our con-stant "becoming." From one moment to the next, we are changing, becoming something we were not before. It is never completed. This process is a creative one that includes our choices, our reactions, our actions, and our thoughts. Some say that every thought we have creates an energy in the universe. Many teachings tell us that every word and every action we make creates ripple effects in the Cosmos. For some, it's called *karma*. Every action has a consequence, which in turn creates a new action and consequence, *ad infinitum*. We create the world with every word and every breath.

As co-creators with the Divine, we have a responsibility for our creations. When we realize that we really do create the world around us in both visible and invisible ways, we understand the awesomeness of that power. Our task, then, is to create well; to create lives worth living for ourselves and others, relationships that celebrate the creative expression of each being, communities that support life, healthy environments that help other beings thrive, and a world that is filled with beauty, love, and justice. If we do this, we are indeed "God's work of art" (Eph. 2:10).

HOW TO BRING CREATIVITY INTO YOUR LIFE

Each day in the morning liturgy we describe God as "mechadesh b'chol yom tamid ma'aseh b'resheit"—the one who "renews daily the work of creation." We human beings are God's partners in the ongoing work of creation. We need to be creative, and God needs our creativity.

RABBI ADINA ALLEN

How we create the stuff of our lives and participate in the ongoing creation of the Cosmos is as infinite and varied as each individual.

While the creative arts are one facet of Creativity, and artistic practice is a wonderful way to explore Creativity, every thought and action of our lives is creative. Our days and nights are filled with Creativity—the continual birthing of the new—if we only see it that way.

YOU ARE AN ARTIST

Over the years, when I talk about creative art as a spiritual practice, I have heard countless people tell me, "I am not an artist" or "I am not creative." I beg to differ. We are all creative, and we can all create art. One does not have to be a professional artist to enjoy painting, making music, dancing, or writing. Matthew Fox explains that we all have permission to create: "Creativity is seen as a spiritual, inwardly-driven activity, directly influenced by a Higher Power, or God. That is the ultimate in inspiration for me: to know I have 'permission' to be creative and to be a creator too."

Years ago, I trained under a visionary teacher, Pat Schneider, who created a process for teaching writing to non-writers called The Amherst Writers and Authors Method. Underlying this practice is the understanding that we are all writers, all artists, regardless of professional training or status. Pat used her method of teaching with virtually illiterate women living in housing projects, and she discovered that given the supportive, safe opportunity to voice their innermost feelings and thoughts on paper, the writing was deeply moving, authentic, healing, and profoundly creative.

When we remove the judgment of being an "artist" or fear of making "bad art," we free ourselves to create that which calls to us from deep within. Whether we are moved by our own emotions or the beauty of the surrounding landscape, we can allow ourselves to express it through a creative art practice of some kind. We can play, explore, experiment. Writing a poem, composing a song, or drawing a portrait allows us to see ourselves as capable of creating, even if we never show our artwork to another soul.

Art is also often a gateway into the subconscious, the psyche, or the True Self, revealing symbols and meanings not always available to our conscious minds. In many traditions, that True Self is none other than the Divine, and art is often considered "divinely inspired." In fact, the word "inspiration," which drives all creativity, comes from the Latin *in spirare*, or "in breath," and breath was synonymous with Spirit. The images and meanings that arise in art practice can give us deep insight into ourselves, the world around us, and our relationship to what we call Divine, as well as guide us toward inspired action in the world.

Suiko McCall, Abbess of The Art Monastery, a New Monastic community, describes the intersection of spirituality, the creative arts, and action in the world this way: "If you reflect quietly and with great compassion, does the clarity of contemplation reveal your passion to be one that would have a truly positive impact on other beings? Will it harm none? Does it allow your creative spirit to take flight with unbounded enthusiasm, providing ongoing inspiration to yourself and to others?"

Like Contemplation, we must come to our art practice regularly and without judgment, expectation, or preconceived ideas of what our art should be. We must simply show up in open receptivity and allow whatever needs to be seen, heard, or spoken to arise. Creativity is a form of play, which is essential for human life. Carl Jung said, "The creative mind plays with the object it loves." This is what Christian pastor Kirk Byron Jones calls "holy play."

We should create for the sheer joy of creating. Whether writing, drawing, taking photographs, making a pot, or making music, the process becomes more important than any product at the end. When we spend time with paint or the piano, playing, without focusing on the outcome, we are tapping into our imaginations, and imagination makes the Cosmos come alive and contributes to the ongoing creation of the universe.

CREATIVITY IN EVERY MOMENT

We do not have to be making "art" to exercise Creativity. Creativity takes many forms. For some, it might be most evident in the work we do, striving to bring our inspiration and imagination to our entrepreneurial business or healing arts practice. For others, it might be in our families, using our imaginations to raise children or care for our elders. For others, it might be one of our hobbies, tending a beautiful flower garden or building a bookshelf. Our imagination knows no bounds, and neither does our Creativity.

If every moment of our lives is an opportunity to create, then it is our mindfulness of that potential that brings the possibility of genuine excitement and enthusiasm for even the most mundane task. If, when I make dinner for my family, I am attentive to the "art" of a lovingly prepared meal and serve it with care, then I bring something into the world that didn't exist before, a moment of shared pleasure and attention that ripples outward. When I talk to a client on the phone, I am aware that I can choose to create goodwill and understanding or disagreement. Both choices can change the world. But if I choose to create a pleasant and productive exchange, I am "bringing the Divine back to the community," as Matthew Fox says.

No matter what we do—whether work or play, from the mundane to the most dramatic—we can do it with attention to Creativity.

Every moment allows us to decide what color, shape, word, or note we want our lives to reflect. What we say, our actions, and even our thoughts are the media we use. We can choose to create from our deepest selves to bring beauty, love, or joy into every moment. One of the principles of biology, as expressed in Biomimicry, is that "Life creates conditions conducive to life." As life, we can choose to create a beautiful, expressive world conducive to life—or not.

BECOMING WHO YOU HAVE ALWAYS BEEN

Rabbi Rami Shapiro describes God as "The Happening that is Happening in All Happenings," or the constant becoming of all becomings, or the force that moves *that which is* into *that which will be.* Like the Divine and the Cosmos itself, all beings are always in the process of becoming, and each moment is a continual creative birthing of the new "self." This is biological as well as spiritual. Every second, new cells are being created in our bodies. Every minute, we have the opportunity to transform, to grow, to enlarge. Julia Cameron, author of *The Artist's Way,* says, "In a sense, as we are creative beings, our lives become our work of art."

What do we choose to become? If we are always becoming, then every choice we make is a part of that process. This means how we respond to the world is always a creative choice. How will we become better people in a better world? Using our imaginations to overcome obstacles or move toward growth is a creative act. How we let go of old patterns and beliefs and are open to what is different, what is new, and what is possible are the very seeds of becoming.

Of course, this is what we have been doing through all Ten Words up until now: Attention, Acceptance, Authenticity, Benevolence,

Balance, and Contemplation have all aided us in transforming ourselves by letting go of old patterns and beliefs and welcoming the new and possible. We are becoming better people.

CREATING A BETTER WORLD

As we move forward into Collaboration, Celebration, and Care, we give birth to ourselves as spiritually-centered beings *acting in the world* from that center. Psychologist Rollo May said, "We express our being by creating. Creativity is a necessary sequel to being." When we choose to align ourselves with our being—who we truly are at the core and which we only discover through inner spiritual attention—we find our authentic voice. Our unique, internal language is then expressed through our creativity in every moment, and we can become the people we imagine ourselves to be in a world that supports the Creativity of all.

Creative energy helps us grow, learn, and change. Our imagination and willingness to seek new or different ways of acting, thinking, or believing enables us to overcome or work through the hard times of our lives. Without the desire for something to change, to become something different, we remain mired in our troubles and patterns. But because we can imagine something different, we begin to make it so.

The same is true for our families, communities, countries, and planet. The very human creative urge is what enables us to have and raise children, build schools and hospitals, playgrounds and parks, businesses and non-profits. Because we can imagine it, we can build it. The world becomes through our imaginations. That means we have a responsibility to create well, to create a better world.

CO-CREATE WITH THE DIVINE

If our Creativity brings the world into existence from moment to moment, we must consider what we are bringing to life. We must ask if we are creating things and moments of beauty and love or hatred and fear. In a spiritual sense, we are not only co-creators but are also in a constant exchange of giving and receiving that which is created and creative. "Creativity is God's gift to us. Using our creativity is our gift back to God," according to Julia Cameron. We extend that to ask, what gift will we choose to give back to God? Perhaps it is a world that supports all beings to thrive.

You are an active participant in your own unfolding.
MICHAEL B. BECKWITH

REFLECTION QUESTIONS

1. What does Creativity mean to me?

2. Why is Creativity important to me?

3. How do I experience Creativity in myself? In others? In the world and cosmos?

4. What prevents me from being creative?

5. Is there a creative art form I enjoy or would like to learn?

6. How can I use a creative art form as a spiritual practice?

7. What else do I do to exercise my creativity?

8. Do I notice that every choice is a creative act? How can I be more aware of what I bring into the world through my choices, words, thoughts, and actions?

9. Do I notice the creativity in the world around me?

10. When I think about "becoming," what do I want to become?

11. How can I share my creativity with my friends, family, neighbors, community, and the world?

SUGGESTED PRACTICES

1. Take a walk in nature and pay attention to what is always in the creative process of becoming. How are the trees constantly becoming themselves, the plants, the animals?

2. Choose an art form you enjoy (or want to learn), and approach it as if it were a spiritual practice.

3. Make a meal as if you are making a work of art.

4. Take a full day to notice your thoughts, words, choices, and actions, and ask what each creates in your life and the world.

5. Think about who you want to become. What would you have to do to become that person?

6. Choose a challenge you are facing and engage your imagination to look for solutions you may not have considered.

7. Imagine the world you want to live in. What can you create to bring that into being?

8

Collaboration

*If reality is a continual process of co-creation between
ourselves and God, as I believe it is, then God is not a
fixed quantity in some cosmic equation. Instead, God
experiments, succeeds, fails, changes, learns, suffers, enjoys,
and grows—just as we do. God yearns for a better world,
pushes against the limits of things, needs us as companions
in this pushing, and gets lonely when we do not respond.*

PARKER J. PALMER

C
o-creation, cooperation, communion, community. These
are the themes of Collaboration. Collaboration is rooted
in the idea that human beings are not just physical entities
but also spiritual beings with a deeper connection to one another
and the universe. If we understand ourselves to be in an interdependent, continually creative, and creating Cosmos, where everything is mutually dependent upon and co-arising and existing with
everything else, then we have no other spiritual option but to collaborate and cooperate with all life and the Divine in the co-creation
of the Cosmos.

Collaboration is an outgrowth of Acceptance and Benevolence. If we can accept ourselves, others, and the world as it is and treat all things with Benevolence, then we will work in concert with it, not against it. We will cooperate instead of competing; we say "Yes, and..." instead of "No." That doesn't mean we don't try to change things so that the world works in more just and fair ways, but when we do engage in change, we come from a place of cooperation, not control or power.

Balance and harmony are also part of Collaboration; the different parts of life must work together to achieve a balanced, harmonious whole. This doesn't always mean equal, but it means that the greater good is the goal. This not only involves cooperation with ourselves, our nature, and our highest values, as well as all of life and the unfolding Cosmos, but also as individuals coming together in communion with a shared purpose to work harmoniously and in unity to achieve common goals.

Ultimately, Collaboration is about relationship. We are in relationship with ourselves, others, the Divine, and the world around us. We explored that relationship in Contemplation, but *how* we live in relationship with everyone and everything is what Collaboration is all about.

We must move from "Me" consciousness and action to "We" consciousness and behavior. That "We" goes beyond family, tribe, nation, or group to "Universal We," or a kind of cosmic consciousness. Contemporary spiritual teacher Adyashanti says simply, "We are birthed into sangha, into sacred community. It is called the world."

WHY IS COLLABORATION IMPORTANT?

If we have no peace, it is because we have
forgotten that we belong to each other.
MOTHER TERESA

In all traditions, we are called to recognize our interdependence with all of life and to live our lives in good relationship to all under creation. The indigenous traditions are especially articulate about this, recognizing that all of life is kin, and we are one "family." These other-than-human kin include mountains and rivers; the elders who are animals, plants, and fungi; the spirits of places and things; planets and stars; deities and unseen kin; and many others whose lives and bodies are entangled with our own. For that reason, we are instructed to treat everyone and everything with the reverence, respect, and reciprocity that exists among relations. As Chief Seattle has said, "Humankind has not woven the web of life. We are but one thread within it. Whatever we do to the web, we do to ourselves. All things are bound together. All things connect."

Buddhism and Daoism also insist that all is interconnected and that beings must work in harmony and balance. Both traditions explain that the lack of cooperation, collaboration, or recognition of our mutual "co-arising" creates imbalance, disease, and misfortune. When we fight against the natural laws of the universe or what is, we create suffering. Conversely, accepting and working "with" reality can alleviate suffering. The Daoist concept of *Wu-Wei*, or "effortless action," is a perfect example of this idea. It is exemplified by the Zhuangzi story of Cook Ding, a butcher who could slice through tough meat effortlessly because he worked with the grain of the meat and the small spaces between bones, not against them.

Even the Abrahamic religions talk about Collaboration, especially the relationship between God and his creation, and the responsibility of human beings to work in communion with each other and with life. It begins in the story of Genesis. God creates all the beings of the earth, and then he creates humans, giving them "dominion" over his creations. Too often, the Biblical idea of "dominion" is taken to mean that one part of life has power or control over another, but dominion really means "responsibility for." In this interpretation, it is said that God gave humans dominion over nature to be His representatives or stewards in caring for the natural world. By that definition, we are responsible for working with each other and all of life as God would.

Because of that idea, the Bible is filled with verses on cooperation, teamwork, unity, and collaboration for the greater good. It's not just Kumbaya or "Let's all get along." The Bible stresses that cooperation is necessary for health, wellness, and community strength. In Ecclesiastes 4:9-12, it is stated that:

> Two are better than one because they have a good return
> for their labor. For if either of them falls, the one will lift
> up his companion. But woe to the one who falls when
> there is not another to lift him up. Furthermore, if two
> lie down together they keep warm, but how can one be
> warm alone? And if one can overpower him who is alone,
> two can resist him. A cord of three strands is not quickly
> torn apart.

Collaboration is also the very basis of the Jewish religion. From the beginning, the covenant between YHWH and the people of Israel is a cooperative agreement. It's a reciprocal arrangement in which YHWH agrees to help Man if Man helps YHWH by living in accordance with the principles of generosity, compassion, and concern for justice and the welfare of others—and not worship other gods.

Many of the laws give specific ways in which that is accomplished, including, for example, rules about the humane treatment of workers and slaves and letting fields lay fallow to regenerate, which is a cooperative relationship with the earth itself. Cooperation and Collaboration are also seen as fundamental to *Tikkun Olam*, or the completion of the world. We must work together, and with God, to gather all the scattered sparks of Divinity back together into a whole.

Islam is also a very collaborative tradition, and many social, economic, and political rules and laws outline ways in which people must cooperate with others, including equality, sharing of profits, and *Zakat*, or mandatory financial care for people in need. Other Islamic principles of Collaboration include equal rights for women and prisoners of war and the collective interest of the community superseding the individual desire for power or gain.

In Hinduism, the concept of Indra's Net, or the web of interdependence and cooperation, is an ancient Vedic teaching. Another Vedic teaching of cooperation and collaboration is *"Paropakaram idham shareeram,"* or the purpose of the human body is to help others. This can be seen in the practice of *seva*, or service, which is part of every Hindu community. Whether through acts of charity, physical support, or care for the temples or the earth, Hinduism asks us to recognize the web of interdependence to collaborate, cooperate, and co-create a world that cares for everyone.

In some way, in all traditions, the Divine itself is seen as the *process* of Collaboration; it's a verb. The Divine is in a constant state of relationship with creation, and we are in relationship with the Divine. That relationship is an active, cooperative, collaborative one that makes life and the Cosmos possible.

Beyond religious traditions, science and social science have also repeatedly shown that the key to survival is relationships, specifically collaborative and cooperative ones, whether we are talking about human beings, trees in a forest, cells in an organism, or the intricate, interdependent web of life on this planet. It goes beyond mere survival, however. Psychotherapist Danil Foor writes, "Learning to navigate these other kinds of relationships is not only a fundamental life skill but also supportive of personal transformation, a source of great joy and intimacy, and the foundation of healthy culture."

HOW TO BRING COLLABORATION INTO YOUR LIFE

Far too often, people think of themselves as just individuals, separated from one another, whereas you are connected, and what you do affects the whole world.

ARCHBISHOP DESMOND TUTU

We have a problem in Western culture: a fundamental belief that the individual is sacrosanct and that the human being is separate from other beings. We have put "Me" before "We." We have placed the "I" in front of everything else. The "selfie" has become our modern icon, said Rabbi Lord Jonathan Sacks.

We believe that we stand alone, that our power lies in competition, conquest, and control of others and our environment, and that needing another is a sign of weakness. If we look around, we can see that ideology in every aspect of our lives, from our relationships with our bodies to our politics and our treatment of the environment. Frankly, it's not working very well. We are more depressed and more unwell, our environment is degraded, and we are at war with each other for power and control. We are on the verge of collapse, all in the name of DIY.

To return to health, happiness, and prosperity, we must return to a proper relationship with the world around us; we must move from the idea of "Me" to "We." We must work "with" not "for" or "against." We must shift from concepts of competition, conquest, and control to collaboration, cooperation, and consideration. We must remember that we are a community of beings in co-creative communion with each other and the Divine.

GET HUMBLE

Humility is the first step. We need each other. We are in relationship with all of life, and one is not greater than the other, but the whole is greater than the parts. Humility is a value held highly by all traditions, and most have sayings that go something like, "Do not put yourself above others."

When we put ourselves above others, we create power structures, dualities, and conflicts that separate us from each other and make communion impossible. When we do, we get politics of personality over polity, wealth at the cost of well-being, offense over morality, and loneliness over love. When we believe we are right and others are wrong, or we are better and others are lesser, there is no way that the process of collaboration, i.e., respect and appreciation for the contributions of others, can occur. In other words, it is only by recognizing an equal relationship, or partnership, that collaboration and cooperation are possible. That is humility.

It's also what we mean when we use the term "self-less." On a deep spiritual level, "selfless" means that our individual sense of separation from all of life is dissolved, and we discover that we are unified with all. However, in this context, it refers to how that experience or knowledge of unity shows up in action. Selflessness is not the negation or repression of our individuality or a false humility that denigrates our contributions but the sublimation of the *supremacy of individuality* in service to the greater good. Rabbi Lord Jonathan Sacks suggested that whenever we say the word "self," we should replace it with "other" and see what changes. When we remember that sometimes we give and other times we receive, we realize that we are in a symbiotic relationship with the world around us. Our "self" and its needs become less important than working to ensure that the collective, or all "selves," get their needs met.

AGAINST VS. WITH

When we talk about Collaboration, we are talking about working "with" ourselves, each other, and the world around us, not "for" or "against." We are not in an adversarial role with ourselves or others; we are not trying to make the world conform to our vision of how it should be by forcing it, nor are we trying to negate anyone's needs or individuality in favor of our own.

In our efforts to make sure everyone's needs are met, we don't need to prod, push, overcome, or punish ourselves or others into being better people. All too often, we think that we can make ourselves or others better through manipulation. We can insist on punishments and rewards or use guilt and shame to get ourselves or others to toe the line.

However, countless research studies in Belongingness Theory have shown that those methods do not work. What works is when people feel truly seen, heard, accepted, and acknowledged and know their contributions are valid and given due consideration. What works is when people feel they are accepted, belong, and are in equal partnership with themselves and others. Collaboration and cooperation require trust.

We develop trust through the practices of Attention, Acceptance, Authenticity, Benevolence, and an expressed interest in the shared purpose of Balance and harmony.

There are endless articles on the internet about how to collaborate with others, but they all have one thing in common: a shared interest in the greater good and a willingness to sublimate the individual ego needs (not individual expression) to the whole.

SCARCITY VS. ABUNDANCE

Often, people believe they need to use competition, conquest, and control to get their needs met because there's only so much to go around. This is a belief in scarcity. When we fear that we will not survive or get what we want if we don't bully and jockey, cajole and conquer, we cannot and will not collaborate. We cannot cooperate, and we cannot form community. What if we changed our belief to one of abundance? What if we trusted that we would have what we need? What if we knew that others' gain or loss had no impact on our own? What if we believed that the Cosmos itself was in a collaborative relationship with us?

For ourselves, we must ask if we are using power, conquest, competition, or control to gain an advantage that might weaken others or whether we are willing to let go of fears so that all might get their needs met. Are we willing to work so *everyone* is happier, healthier, and more fulfilled? Are we willing to see that the abundance of another in no way reduces our own?

Likewise, are we willing to see where our needs are being met without having to use power? All traditions use words such as "grace" or "love" to express the truth that the Cosmos or the Divine does provide for our needs, with no manipulation necessary. For no reason other than that we are alive, we receive the abundance of life. This is where our practices of gratitude become important. If we can see that we receive constantly, we can rest there with deep gratitude. Aren't we lucky?

RIGHT VS. RIGHT

What is right? What is wrong? Questions of morality form the basis of most spiritual traditions. We explored morality in Benevolence, and we discovered that according to most traditions, what is Benevolent is most often less harmful to self or others than the alternatives.

Moral questioning is also an important aspect of Collaboration but has a slightly different nuance. This time, harm isn't the only barometer for what is kind or right. We must consider not only what is right for me or another but what is right for the whole. Is what is right for me *also* right for others *and* the whole? In other words, through Collaboration, we move from zero-sum games with individual winners or losers to a non-zero-sum game in which the net benefit or net loss to the whole system is considered.

This plays out in every relationship of our lives. Is what is right for me in my marriage also right for my partner and the marriage? Is what is right for me in my work also right for the clients and the company? Is what is right for me in any situation also right for others and the greater whole? And on and on.

This question is the very basis of the concept of Collaboration. It's not easy. Questions of morality are rarely black and white; sometimes, as we have seen, what might appear right is not right in the larger sense. However, without exploring the question of rightness for the whole, we are not truly collaborating or cooperating; we are manipulating others to get our needs met at whatever cost.

EITHER/OR VS. BOTH/AND

Essentially, Collaboration means that we must let go of our self-importance to recognize that we are all interdependent and that every action must be considered through the lens of "both/and." It must be seen as "I get my needs met, *and* you do, too, and if we all get our needs met, the whole is stronger." That's how we move from "Me" consciousness to "We" consciousness. It's also how we collaborate. After all, no one person or entity can decide what is ultimately right for the whole.

The Quakers have a unique way of coming to decide what is the best "both/and." When they meet to make decisions that affect the whole meeting or group, they do not go for consensus because that often means a stronger person or group overpowers a smaller or less vocal one. Instead, they seek the "Sense of the Meeting," a form of communal discernment. It's not a democratic process in terms of voting, but the group waits until all people who might have something to add have spoken, and then they listen contemplatively for what is ultimately "right" for the whole. If nothing anyone contributed carries the "sense" of what is right, they wait until something does.

Using this kind of collaborative process takes time, but the net result is that one party doesn't feel disempowered or overpowered because the whole group is focused on what is best for the whole. Usually, everyone agrees, and no one is unhappy with the result, not because they have been controlled or cajoled into it, but because it seems like the best possible solution for everyone. It's always "both/and."

COMMUNION AND COMMUNITY

Communion is a word often used in spiritual traditions, and it means a kind of merging or being of one heart and mind. While that has spiritual power in the sense of communion with the Divine, in Collaboration, we are more interested in Community; it is in community with others that we sense communion.

In community, the desire is to be in relationship with others, with life. We all have the same intention: to partner with one another. That is the single heart and mind of communion. That partnership does not mean merging into a single, undifferentiated mass but acknowledging our differences as *integral* and vital to the whole.

Collaboration acknowledges and celebrates difference. Nothing in the Cosmos is homogenous; the community of all life is infinitely diverse. It is precisely because we are different that we contribute in unique ways to the ongoing co-creation of the Cosmos. A tree is different than a flower, but one is no less important to the landscape than the other. We need and want both, and it is the interplay between and within diversity that, for many, is the Divine's collaborative expression itself.

Many of us aspire for community, but we build community by recognizing our diversity and interdependence and the actions of collaboration and cooperation. In community, we find communion by opening our hearts to each other to know and be known, to understand and be understood, to love and be loved in all our uniqueness. This means that we pass from theory to practice and that we can persevere together through trials, joys, and sufferings. This is the essence and reward of Collaboration.

THE DIVINE AS LIFE-PARTNER

Ultimately, the exploration of Collaboration leads us to discover that we are in a collaborative, co-creative relationship with the Divine. Contrary to popular belief, the Divine doesn't discriminate; the Divine isn't interested in who wins or who loses. The Divine isn't an "either/or" proposition; the Divine is "both/and." The Divine wants life to live, which means that all life must cooperate and collaborate with each other and the Divine itself and that the Divine is collaborating with life.

We, as life partners with Divine life-ing, must work "with," not "for" or "against," and consider what is best for Life, not just for our life or the lives of others, but Life as a whole. Christian mystic Hildegard of Bingen understood this when she said, "Everything that is in the heavens, on earth, and under the earth is penetrated with connectedness, penetrated with relatedness."

This is when we begin to explore our own relationship with the Divine. Who or what are we partnering with? What kind of partner or collaborator is the Divine? What kind of partner do we choose to be? Do we choose to fight against the Divine or its expressions, flaunting our *hubris* to tell the Divine how to do life? Or do we choose to work with the processes the Divine offers? After all, as we have seen, if we don't cooperate and collaborate, we end up in a world filled with misery, despair, and destruction. We end up without life.

We are caught in an inescapable network of mutuality,
tied in a single garment of destiny. Whatever
affects one directly, affects all indirectly.

REV. DR. MARTIN LUTHER KING, JR.

REFLECTION QUESTIONS

1. What does Collaboration mean to me?

2. Why is Collaboration important to me?

3. Where in my life do I experience Collaboration? Where do I not?

4. What prevents me from Collaboration?

5. How can I cooperate and collaborate instead of fighting with myself?

6. Where can I collaborate and cooperate with others?

7. How can I collaborate and cooperate with my environment?

8. How can I collaborate and cooperate with the world?

9. What kind of relationship do I want to have with the Divine?

10. How can I collaborate with all of life?

SUGGESTED PRACTICES

1. In your contemplation or daily life, explore interdependence. Take notice of how things in the world or your life are dependent on other things or people.

2. Practice seeing how your needs are met by others and the world around you. Practice gratitude for those gifts.

3. Practice seeing how you meet the needs of others and the world around you.

4. In any situation in which you have the option to control or collaborate, explore what happens if you drop the need to control. What do you need to do?

5. In any situation with others, imagine that you are equals trying to solve a problem. Invite others to share their thoughts and ideas and be willing to let your own ideas change as a result. Look for the win/win and choose that!

6. Throughout the day, ask yourself, "If I were looking to support the greater good here, what would I do/say?"

9

Celebration

In the end, the universe can only be explained in terms of celebration: It is an exuberant expression of existence itself.

THOMAS BERRY

To celebrate has many meanings: to perform rites or rituals or to mark a special occasion with festivities or solemn acts. It also means to praise or to honor. Within those functional definitions, there is something even deeper. Celebration is the expression of joy. It is a higher octave of Acceptance, combined with Creativity and Collaboration. When we accept what is and allow ourselves to be awed by it, to recognize the incredible diversity of the Cosmos, the infinite creativity of the Divine, the boundless bounty all around us, and the deeply shared experience of all life, we can only respond with exuberant joy.

In all traditions, that joy is expressed through ritual or worship. Through songs of praise, dances, prayers, music, feasts, liturgical rites, or rituals, we express our joy and gratitude for our gifts and for being alive. Even in the absence of traditional forms, we can experience the joy of Celebration every day: when we greet a beautiful sunrise, stunned by the colors; when we hold our lover's face, ecstatic; when we see a child laugh and play, reminded of the sheer pleasure of life; when we accomplish a hard task; when we see the full moon rise in all its glory. Even in darker moments, when we experience the compassion of another human being or remember that even within pain and suffering, there is life, we are in the realm of Celebration.

At its heart, Celebration arises from the sense of wonder and awe. To celebrate is to elevate each moment to something wondrous, something awesome, something worth being alive for. Each moment gives us the opportunity to feel joy for the simple fact of existence. For, as Berry has said, the universe itself is a Celebration; it is the "exuberant expression of existence."

WHY IS CELEBRATION IMPORTANT?

Be cheerful with joyous celebration in every
season of life. Let your joy overflow!
PHILIPPIANS 4:4-7

In every tradition, celebrating with joy is not just common but required. The Torah and Bible are filled with feasts and celebrations. From Genesis to the Book of Revelation, over and over, the people are told to rejoice and celebrate—and they do. There are feasts and celebrations for all kinds of special occasions, with instructions for food, drink, prayers, relaxation, and revelry.

In Judaism, there are the celebrations for Sabbath, Passover, Chanukah, and Purim, to name just a few. In Christianity, there is Christmas, Easter, Saint's Days, and Ash Wednesday, among many. Each of these celebrations commemorates some event in the life of the Jewish people or Jesus and his followers, and even if they are mournful occasions, there is cause to celebrate through song, ritual, and gathering. But perhaps the most important reason for celebrating in the Judeo-Christian tradition is simply because today is a good day to celebrate. As Psalm 118:24 says, "This is the day which the Lord has made; Let us rejoice and be glad in it."

In Islam, there are two great celebrations, or *Eids*. *Eid-ul-Fitr* signifies the completion of the Holy Month of Ramadan, and *Eid-ul-Adha* follows the completion of the annual Hajj pilgrimage. These celebrations are primarily gatherings of prayer to celebrate Allah's bounty and greatness after a period of hardship (Ramadan and the Hajj are physically demanding) and include performing good deeds by supporting the poor and needy. Of course, there is often food and gatherings at these festivals, but the essence of these celebrations is the remembrance of awe, worship of Allah, joy, and gratitude for life.

Hinduism is filled with celebration. There are the formal celebrations of *Holi* (Festival of Colors), *Diwali* (Festival of Lights), and *Dussehra* (Festival of Triumph), all of which are multi-day spectacles filled with food, dance, music, processions, and more, but there are also countless *pujas*, feast and celebration days for different deities, and other commemorations. Sometimes, it can seem that every day is a celebration in Hindu communities. In fact, that is the point. *Ananda*, which means "joy from all sides," or bliss, is a central concept in Hinduism, and Brahman, or the Divine, is referred to as *Anandobrahma,* or bliss itself. In other words, our very nature (and the nature of the Divine) is joy! Why not celebrate that?

Buddhists and Daoists are a little more restrained in their expressions of celebration, but there are also many elaborate holidays, rituals, and liturgies that celebrate the life of the Buddha or special days for Daoist deities and are filled with processions, flowers, candles, house cleaning, and temple visits. One of the most important Buddhist celebrations is *Parinirvana Day*, which celebrates the Buddha's death. It is a joyful occasion in which temples are filled with offerings because Buddhists believe that upon his death, the Buddha was freed from the world of suffering and achieved full enlightenment, or *Nirvana*, defined as a state of bliss or joy due to freedom from the endless cycle of rebirth. That is the goal of Buddhist practice, so of course, it's worth celebrating.

In all traditions and cultures, we celebrate rites of passage: births, deaths, puberty, weddings, graduations, and initiations, or any number of life cycle events that mark a transition from one state or status to another. Simply arriving at the milestone is worth celebrating. Remember that not long ago, our lives were far more fragile; many people never made it past childhood. In Judaism, there is a prayer that expresses this type of celebration: "Blessed are You, Adonai our God, Sovereign of all, who has given us life, sustained us, and brought us to this moment." Hallelujah! We made it to NOW!

In our secular lives, we celebrate everything from closing a deal to the first day of school, from a winning game to buying a new car. We celebrate Mother's Day, Father's Day, Children's Day, Valentine's Day, and other non-religious holidays. National or collective holidays celebrate battle victories and legal ones or honor the accomplishments of heroes, real or imagined. We raise our glasses in toast at gatherings with friends and throw parties to celebrate weekends. In other words, we celebrate almost everything.

However, Rabbi Abraham Joshua Heschel reminds us that there is a difference between celebrating and entertainment. He says, "People of our time are losing the power of celebration. Instead of celebrating, we seek to be amused or entertained. Celebration is an active state, an act of expressing reverence or appreciation. To be entertained is a passive state—it is to receive pleasure afforded by an amusing act or a spectacle... Celebration is a confrontation, giving attention to the transcendent meaning of one's actions."

Celebration is what we humans do. We could say that to celebrate is to be human. It seems to be fundamental to who we are. Neuroscientists say that we are hardwired for joy (not happiness, that's different). We experience joy simply because we know we are alive, and it is meaningful for us.

In other words, we are conscious of our existence and, thus, naturally celebrate it for the miracle it is. This is why mystics claim that our ability to experience joy is proof of the Infinite, or Consciousness itself. As the Christian monk and mystic Pierre Teilhard de Chardin explains, "Joy is the infallible sign of the presence of God." When we are joyful, we are expressions of the Divine's joy in existence. God is having a party of life, and we're invited.

Our ability to empathize with and care for each other is also an expression of the Divine and something to be celebrated. We are capable of kindness, friendship, forgiveness, compassion, and love. We can celebrate our curiosity and creativity, intellect, physical capabilities, and ability to wonder at the universe. We can celebrate our friends and families, the successes of others, and the myriad ways we inspire and are inspired by each other.

We can even celebrate our hard times, how we come together to support one another in grief and pain, or the fact that our suffering often brings wisdom. In grief, we celebrate the love we had for what we lost. In other words, to be human is to experience life in all its colors and potential. This alone is worth celebrating: the awe of being alive and the thrill of discovering what it means to be human.

HOW TO BRING CELEBRATION INTO YOUR LIFE

Each day holds a surprise. But only if we expect it can we see, hear, or feel it when it comes to us. Let's not be afraid to receive each day's surprise, whether it comes to us as sorrow or as joy. It will open a new place in our hearts, a place where we can welcome new friends and celebrate more fully our shared humanity.

HENRI J.M. NOUWEN

Celebration can take many forms. At its heart, it is any action that expresses joy, gratitude, or acknowledgment of the magic and mystery of life or the Divine. There is an element of reverence, whether exuberant or quiet.

Years ago, I had a friend who had a stroke. It affected the part of her brain that allows for complex speech, so she could only say two words, "F#*k!" and "Wow!" She spent her time gazing around with wonder and awe, mostly silent, but when she spoke, she repeated those two words over and over. Though I suspected she could be expressing frustration at her situation, I preferred to think that she had somehow glimpsed the mystery and beauty of life itself and was in deep celebration and reverence. I thought it was brilliant. What else do you really need to say, except maybe "Thank you"?

In her book, *Help. Thanks. Wow.: The Three Essential Prayers*, writer Anne Lamott explains that taking the time to acknowledge, appreciate, and be thankful for the gifts of life is key to getting through hard times and moving forward with joy. Through the many ways we celebrate ourselves, others, and the world around us, we turn our attention with reverence to that which is life-nourishing, feels good, connects us to others and the Divine, and reminds us that life itself is worth living.

FORMAL CELEBRATION AND RITUAL

As we have seen, all traditions have formal times for celebrating — communal gatherings that bring people together to honor, worship, or express gratitude and joy through special actions. Whether we choose to celebrate the holidays and festivals of specific traditions or make up our own, it is important to set aside times for formal celebration of some kind.

There are many opportunities for formal celebration. In addition to religious holidays and rites of passage, some cultures celebrate the seasons in special ways. For example, solstices, equinoxes, full moons, mid-summer, harvest, or the first days of spring are often set aside for feasts, worship, and celebrations. Others choose specific dates that are meaningful, such as birthdays, death days, anniversaries, etc. And still, others celebrate on days that have mythic or narrative significance. In truth, there is something to celebrate every day of the year.

Celebrations can take place in the home or temples or churches, in the streets, in other sacred places, and even virtually. In all cases, however, there is some kind of ritual to mark the occasion: symbolic actions that create sacred space and time and allow us to experience an elevated moment. The ritual elements also create a connection to the Divine, however defined. That is the point of ritual: to foster the relationship between ourselves and the world of the sacred, to remember that we are part of a larger process, and to acknowledge and celebrate that connection.

Rituals can be elaborate multi-day events filled with pageantry and prayer or very simple: a special meal, a recitation, or lighting a candle each morning and silently acknowledging one's gratitude or joy. Each culture has its own ritual practices, but they all have certain things in common, including the use of elements of the natural and spiritual world, food, drink, song, prayer, or dance. Most importantly, rituals are not spontaneous; there is a defined order for the proceeding.

Choosing specific times to celebrate through ritual adds a rhythm to life, reminding us, when we get busy with our daily activities, to pause, gather with friends and family, or simply take the time for ourselves to acknowledge and celebrate the beauty and mystery of life, and the relationship we have with the Divine. Whether our rituals are private or include others, it's important to set aside time to acknowledge and celebrate our connection to the Divine and to Life. Maybe our ritual is as simple as the Hebrew toast, "*L'Chaim*"—To life!

CELEBRATE YOURSELF

The second of the Ten Words, Acceptance, includes self-acceptance, or allowing ourselves to be exactly who we are, just as we are. However, to celebrate ourselves is to take that one step further. It's not just to accept and allow, but to appreciate our uniqueness, strengths, and weaknesses; our failures as much as our successes; our ups as well as our downs; our good ideas as much as our not-so-good ones; to joyfully celebrate our wholeness (holiness). "I celebrate myself, and sing myself," wrote American poet Walt Whitman. To celebrate our self is to welcome and affirm "every atom belonging to me," he exclaims.

Even if we can't yet bring ourselves to celebrate our messy, beautiful wholeness, we can celebrate that we have the gift of life and are given the opportunity to experience all that life has to offer. We can sing and shout for joy simply because we are living, breathing, magnificently complex, and improbable beings, each with our own genius and our own paths...no matter where they might take us. Isn't that worth celebrating?

CELEBRATE OTHERS

The same is true for all other beings. Beyond simply accepting one another, we can celebrate our diversity and the infinite ways life shows up in the Cosmos. American philosopher, poet and Civil Rights activist Audre Lorde said, "It is not our differences that divide us. It is our inability to recognize, accept, and celebrate those differences." Instead of focusing on our differences as negative or threatening, we can celebrate how those differences weave a one-of-a-kind tapestry of life full of color, depth, and variety.

We can also celebrate the way we show up for one another. When someone shows kindness, patience, or forgiveness, we can applaud. When our friends or families go out of their way to do something for another, or even when a total stranger lets us go ahead in line, we can say thank you for the gift. Isn't it amazing that we have the capacity for these things? And isn't it even more amazing when we use that capacity?

If someone displays kindness, compassion, creativity, humility, collaboration, or any other quality that makes the world a better place, we would all be better off if we celebrate that with great joy. Maybe then, it would spread. As Br. David Stendahl-Rast says, "In every joy which kindness triggers, flashes a flicker of that wild joy of limitless belonging."

Too often, however, we belittle or denigrate others' efforts or contributions. We see another's success as somehow reducing our own or another's talents as somehow diminishing ours. We don't celebrate our limitless belonging. What if we could celebrate each other's successes, talents, attempts, and offers as absolutely welcome additions to the whole? Even if they aren't perfect, can we celebrate everyone's efforts and contributions as gifts that make the world so much richer? We don't need to wait for perfection to celebrate. We can honor and praise every step of the way.

Imagine if, in each interaction, we met one another with the intent to celebrate the being before us. Simply by acknowledging the divine spark of life in the other, we celebrate its existence. Look! Another wonderful example of the Creativity and Collaboration of life! In many indigenous cultures, it is said that each being has its own song. Can we hear the song each being sings of itself, rejoicing in its sound...and maybe even sing along?

FIND JOY EVERY DAY

The Sufi poet Rumi wrote a famous poem, "The Guest House," in which he describes the human being as the proprietor of a guesthouse, welcoming each thought, feeling, and experience, whether good or bad, as a guest bringing gifts from the Divine. This is the essence of finding joy in every moment: seeing everything as a gift worth welcoming and celebrating.

Of course, this isn't always easy, especially when things are hard. In some cases, it might feel impossible. We don't always know why we or others must endure difficult times, and we can despair. The challenge in celebrating each moment is remembering that everything has something to offer us, even if it's just to show us that we are strong enough to get through it.

Finding joy in life also helps us navigate the hard times. Joy is the raft that carries us across the sea of suffering. Archbishop Desmond Tutu, who certainly knew about suffering and joy, says, "As we discover more joy, we can face suffering in a way that ennobles rather than embitters. We have hardships without becoming hard. We have heartbreaks without becoming broken." We can face whatever comes without letting it knock us down by cultivating our ability to find moments of joy and celebration, even in the darkest times.

BE GRATEFUL

This is where practices of gratitude come in. Gratitude or praise is part of Celebration and fundamental to every tradition. It's easy to be grateful and joyful when good things happen, but it's hard to say "Thank you" when bad things happen. It's worth trying, however. Meister Eckhart wrote, "If the only prayer you ever say is 'Thank You,' it's enough." You don't have to know who or what you are thanking, but having the humility to say "Thank you" for the myriad gifts of every day is essential. It keeps us from entitlement or, worse, demand.

Many people say that the more they practice expressing gratitude, the more good things come their way. Keeping a gratitude journal, a gratitude jar, or even a nightly recounting of what you are grateful for is a good start for celebrating through gratitude. Of course, the more you see and celebrate the gifts you receive, the more they appear to multiply! It's where you place your attention. If you are paying attention to each moment as a gift, each moment becomes something worth celebrating.

CELEBRATE LIFE

A good motto is the title of a book written by a friend, *Here for the Joy!* What if we turned our attention with reverence to the joy available to us in every moment, every interaction, every thought, feeling, taste, and experience, no matter what? What if we are here to experience and celebrate the joy of all of it? This is the overwhelming joy mystics write about. When the desire to celebrate, sing, and dance overtakes them, they fall to their knees in praise and awe, exclaiming, "Wow!"

Be not lax in celebrating.
Be not lazy in the festive service of God.
Be ablaze with enthusiasm.
Let us be an alive, burning offering before the altar of God.
HILDEGARD OF BINGEN

REFLECTION QUESTIONS

1. What does Celebration mean to me?

2. Why is Celebration important to me?

3. What events or holidays do I regularly celebrate? How do I celebrate them?

4. What prevents me from celebrating?

5. What brings me joy? How do I express that?

6. What parts of me do I have a hard time celebrating? What prevents me from celebrating all aspects of myself?

7. How can I celebrate myself?

8. How can I celebrate others?

9. Do I practice gratitude regularly? In what ways?

10. How can I find moments of awe and joy every day?

SUGGESTED PRACTICES

1. Make a list of all the events/holidays you celebrate. Which ones are meaningful for you? If they aren't, how can you make them more meaningful? What would you like to celebrate that you don't?

2. Make a list of what brings you joy. How can you celebrate those things?

3. Make a list of all the things you can celebrate about yourself. Each time one of those things arises (or you notice), practice honoring, praising, and celebrating it.

4. Each time you meet someone (or a non-human being), say a silent "I celebrate/honor/praise your existence" to yourself (or aloud, if you are so inclined). Note how that changes your interaction.

5. For one day, practice saying "thank you" to every moment, every thought, the sun, the moon, the birds, the parking space, the dirty dishes, etc. Explore how that makes you feel.

6. Keep a gratitude journal in which you write everything you are grateful for each day. Or create a gratitude jar. Take an empty jar, and every time there is something to be grateful for, write it down and put it in. Then, in a celebration, you can empty it out or read them all, reveling in your good fortune!

7. Put on your favorite dance music and move! Sing in the shower! Spin around! Fall on the grass! Jump for joy!

10

Care

We only care for the things we love. Love everything.

LAURYN AXELROD

Every tradition emphasizes Care as the highest aspect of spiritual life and goes to great lengths to teach us how to care for each other and our world. Whether described as charity, hospitality, service, selflessness, or generosity, Care includes, but goes beyond, the attitudes of compassion, concern, or empathy. Care is those attitudes expressed through action. It is how we take our spirituality off the mat and into real practice. It is how we embed and embody our practice in action. We honestly can't say that we are living spiritual lives if we don't care—and we don't show it.

As the culmination of all the previous Ten Words, we bring all our work thus far to the practice of Care. Caring arises from Attention, Acceptance, Authenticity, Benevolence, Balance, Contemplation, Creativity, Collaboration, and Celebration. Whether we are caring for ourselves, others, or the world around us, we only do so through practicing everything we have been cultivating.

At the same time, to care is to come full circle because to care also means "to attend to." When we attend to something, we care about and take care of it. Isn't giving one's full attention to something the most generous act of care? And doesn't it generate the feeling of love? Care, then, is really nothing more or less than love in action, and in many traditions, love is the truest attribute of the Divine.

Care can be as small as taking a spider outside instead of stomping on it or calling to check on a sick friend. It can also be more expansive, such as working to end homelessness or to save the environment. Big or small, every action of Care has a positive impact on the wider world. When we care about something enough, it can inspire us to take action that makes the world a better place. This can lead to a more just and equitable society. When we consider how we act in the world from our spiritual center, it must come from the practice of Care. Likewise, if we care, we must act.

WHY IS CARE IMPORTANT?

As human beings, we each have a responsibility to care for humanity. Expressing concern for others brings inner strength and deep satisfaction. As social animals, human beings need friendship, but friendship doesn't come from wealth and power, but from showing compassion and concern for others.

HH THE 14TH DALAI LAMA

Care makes the world work. When we look around, we can see that when people care about others and the world around them, life is good; people and the planet thrive. When we don't care about others and the world around us, we see the results: war, hate, suffering, environmental devastation, and destruction. For this reason, every tradition makes Care, and the actions that express it, paramount.

In the Abrahamic traditions, care for others is central. In the Torah and Talmud, Jews are taught repeatedly to care for the poor, the hungry, the homeless, the stranger, and the oppressed. As it is said in Psalm 82:3-4, "Defend the poor and the orphan; deal justly with the poor and the destitute. Rescue the weak and the needy; deliver them from the hand of the wicked."

The story told in the Passover *Haggadah* clearly states that if anyone is oppressed, we are all oppressed, and it is the Jewish duty to fight for the oppressed everywhere. There are also many instructions for how to care for the land and its workers, how to harvest fields so that the hungry can eat, and even for animals. *Tzedakah*, or generous giving of money or goods to help others, is part of every Jewish Sabbath, and philanthropy is considered a *mitzvah*, or good deed, for it is taught in Isaiah 32:17, "The work of *tzedakah* shall bring peace."

Likewise, in Christianity. Jesus taught his followers to care for one another and the neediest and least privileged among them. His example and teachings showed others how to care for the sick, feed the poor, and show love, forgiveness, and compassion to all. In many ways, Jesus taught the highest form of Care is service. For Jesus, Care is an act of love. As he said: "My command is this: Love each other as I have loved you" (John 15:12). That means take care of each other.

For this reason, Christians the world over engage in acts of service, whether feeding the poor or tending to orphans, the homeless, the sick, or the needy. Countless Christian charities and NGOs, soup kitchens, and hospitals are sharing and caring the world over. We have the stories of Mother Teresa and St. Francis of Assisi as examples, but there are numbers of nameless Christians doing their best to care for others in ways big and small.

In Islam, The Prophet Mohammad, PBUH, is described as a deeply caring person. In the Qur'an, he is introduced this way: "There certainly has come to you a messenger from among yourselves. He is concerned by your suffering, anxious for your well-being, and gracious and merciful to the believers" (Surah At-Tawbah, 9:128). Through the teachings, Muslims are encouraged to live with the example of The Prophet and treat others with care.

The Qur'an and the Hadith are filled with examples of how to care for others. Care for widows and orphans is emphasized, as is the care for the whole community of Islam. One of the ways Muslims offer care is through *Zakat*, or the giving of alms. As one of the Five Pillars of Islam, *Zakat* requires that every Muslim offer a percentage of their income to the care and support of others. In this way, Muslims fulfill the imperative to care for all members of the *Umma*, or community.

The entire teaching of Buddhism is centered on Care through one thing: the end of suffering. Since suffering is everywhere, it is the Buddhist's obligation to end suffering through the practice of the dharma. The Dalai Lama has repeatedly said that he has one religion: compassion. In Buddhism, compassion is the expression of Care. In Mahayana Buddhism, the highest form of Care is the *Boddhisatva*, one who forgoes their enlightenment to support the enlightenment, or the end of suffering, of others.

In Hinduism, the concepts of *ahimsa*, non-harm, and *karma*, or the law of cause and effect, are central to the practice of Care. One must always be mindful of the consequences of actions, thoughts, and words so as not to cause harm or create negative karma for oneself or others. The giving of charity is constant, and the ritual feeding of the poor, animals, and *sannyasi* is common at temples and festivals.

Likewise, the concept of *seva*, or service, is part of every Hindu's life. The Vedic teachings stress the interdependence of all and the importance of each person performing their duty to others through acts of care. Ancient texts even outlined the specific forms of care each person should take, whether it was taking care of animals, children, the physical needs of the community, or the spiritual teachers. In this way, everyone cared for everyone else, and all needs were met within the community.

The same is true for Sikhs, whose communities are built entirely around the principles of *Sarbat de Bhalla* or working toward the common good of all. For Sikhs, this means reaching out to serve and uplift all of humanity as an expression of devotion to the Creator. The teaching of *Vand Ke Chakna* means to share and support the whole community. Sikhs are required to give 10 percent of their earnings to charity, help in the free kitchens that Sikh communities run, and practice *seva*, or selfless service. For this reason, many Sikh communities are almost completely self-sufficient because everyone cares for everyone in whatever way necessary, whether as doctors, teachers, cooks, dishwashers, or farmers.

All indigenous traditions teach that caring for all beings is required because we are all dependent upon one another for survival. We are inseparably interconnected, so the care of one is the care of all. White Buffalo Calf Woman passed on these instructions from the Lakota Sioux for living and caring.

> Friend, do it this way—that is, whatever you do in life,
> do the very best you can with both your heart and minds.

And if you do it that way, the Power of the Universe will come to your assistance, if your heart and mind are in Unity. When one sits in the Hoop of the People, one must be responsible because All of Creation is related. And the hurt of one is the hurt of all. And the honor of one is the honor of all. And whatever we do affects everything in the universe. If you do it that way—that is, if you truly join your heart and mind as One—whatever you ask for, that's the way it's going to be.

HOW TO BRING CARE INTO YOUR LIFE

Nobody cares how much you know, until
they know how much you care.
THEODORE ROOSEVELT

It's very simple. To care means we must step out of ourselves and our concerns long enough to truly see another and their needs and do what we can to help them meet those needs. We must get out of our heads and into our hearts; we must allow ourselves to be heartbroken at the suffering of others and do what we can to bring an end to that suffering.

Even in the absence of suffering, we must simply hold on to the desire that others have the same opportunity to thrive as we do and then do what we can to make that possible. That means if my friend needs to talk about something that has upset her, I listen and offer support because I know she is hurting. If my neighbor needs help hauling a fallen tree off his driveway, I lend a hand because he might get hurt if he tries to do it himself. If my partner comes home late, tired, and hungry, I will have dinner waiting because I care about their well-being. And if a stranger on the street asks for a few coins, I give what I have in my pocket because it might help. Care means that if I can do something that aids someone's ability to thrive or relieves their suffering, I do it.

WE NATURALLY CARE

We don't need to make ourselves do this. We do it all the time without thinking. In their book, *How Can I Help?* Ram Dass and Paul Gorman note:

> …helping happens simply in the way of things. It's not something we really think about, merely the instinctive response of an open heart. Caring is a reflex. Someone slips, your arm goes out. A car is in a ditch, you join others and push. A colleague at work has the blues, you let her know you care. It all seems natural and appropriate. You live, you help.

Like all the other Ten Words, Care will simply arise from our intention and awareness. However, we must distinguish between helping and fixing versus Care. When we try to help or fix, we come from a position of power; we are stronger, and the other is weaker. That's not Care; it's control. When we come from the place of care or service, we are equals, simply offering what we can from our wholeness (holiness) in the service of the wholeness (holiness) of another.

As Rachel Naomi Remen, MD, says, "Helping, fixing, and serving represent three different ways of seeing life. When you help, you see life as weak. When you fix, you see life as broken. When you serve, you see life as whole. Fixing and helping may be the work of the ego, service the work of the soul."

If we express Care to make ourselves feel better or righteous, that's another red flag. Yes, caring does feel good, but that's not why we do it. It's just a nice byproduct. If we are motivated to care to remove our own discomfort or pain, that's not Care, either. That's bypassing. Care must come from the simple, natural desire that others, no matter what, thrive. The specifics of how they thrive aren't our decision or within our control. We just need to listen carefully for what others need and do that, or, if we can't, do what we can to assist others in doing it for themselves.

CARING FOR OTHERS

There are as many ways to care for others as there are people. Every day offers us an infinite number of possibilities to show Care. We already do it. From the simplest action, such as tucking a child into bed at night, to the grandest, perhaps putting one's life on the line by serving in the military to protect others, we give of ourselves so that others may thrive.

There is no wrong way to show genuine Care, and there are a million right ways. Jesuit priest and mystic Pierre Teilhard de Chardin said, "The most satisfying thing in life is to have been able to give a large part of oneself to others." For many, caring for others is what gives life meaning and purpose. In fact, all the great traditions would say that Care is the whole point of all their teachings.

In his book *48 Ways to Love and Be Loved*, Rabbi Noah Weinberg says, "Some people say, 'I can only give to someone I love.' This is wrong. The Hebrew word for 'give,' *hav*, is the same root as *ahava*, meaning 'love.' The Jewish idea is that giving is what leads to love. When I give to you, I have invested a part of myself in you. You then become more precious to me, and I love you more."

It would then follow that I would continue to give as an expression of love. When we love, we truly want for others what they want for themselves. Everyone ultimately wants to be happy, healthy, and thriving, and if we love, we want that for them, too. That doesn't mean we have to make their lives perfect, but it means that we do what we can to support that desire and that giving both expresses and generates love.

In other words, caring for others is a loving relationship. I like to say that the four most important words in any relationship are, "What do you need?" Instead of assuming we know what the other person or being needs, we must ask. That's an act of respect and love. We must trust that the other can tell us what they need to thrive and then do that! We must let go of thinking we know what is best for anyone or anything else.

It's not always our job to meet the needs of others. Sometimes, we can best express Care by assisting others in getting their needs met themselves. As the saying goes, "If you give a man a fish, he eats for a day. If you teach him to fish, he eats for the rest of his life." It's not always within our capacity to meet others' needs, but we might have the capacity to point them toward getting their needs met elsewhere.

Recently, I heard a story from a friend who was approached by another woman seeking refuge from an abusive marriage. My friend couldn't give the woman shelter in her home at the moment but spent several hours helping her reach the local women's shelter, where she was able to find safe refuge and begin the process of healing.

Caring about others builds trust. By expressing empathy, compassion, love, and understanding through action, we create a sense of belonging and connection with those around us. Through Care, we build community. We break down the walls of separation and cultivate that sense of interdependence necessary for life to work. We have a saying where I live in Vermont. "If your barn falls down, your neighbors will all be there to help." There's something about the recognition that we're all in this together that makes people care. Tragedy can befall anyone; it could be you next time, and you will need your neighbors. This is how we all thrive.

Another important part of caring is doing so without expectation of gain or reward. We give because it's just the thing to do. If we are doing it for our egos—praise or gain—then it's not really Care; we are using others for our needs. At the same time, by caring for others, we find a sense of purpose and fulfillment that goes beyond our own personal interests. Archbishop Desmond Tutu said, "When you are kind to someone else, you end up being joyful, but why? Because we realize that we are made for goodness."

SELF-CARE

A passage in the Dhammapada, Buddhism's fundamental scripture, states: "Don't give up your own welfare/For the sake of others' welfare, however great/Clearly know your own welfare/And be intent on the highest good." As much as we need to express care to others, we must also care for ourselves. We cannot exhaust ourselves trying to care for everyone and everything. Caregiver burnout is real. Compassion fatigue is real. We can spend so much of our time and energy caring for others at our own expense that we end up wrecking ourselves and are too worn out to care for others. That's not Care. That's martyrdom.

To avoid martyrdom, we must care for ourselves as much as for others so we can care for others most effectively. We need to know when we have reached a point of overwhelm or when we simply cannot be present for others in a healthy way. We need to develop routines of self-care that are not about distraction or indulgence but truly give ourselves time to rest, replenish, and restore.

Bubble baths, a glass of wine, or a silly movie can offer temporary relief, but tending to ourselves—caring for ourselves—means knowing what we need to be our best selves in the world. That might mean giving ourselves time to rest or doing things that make us happy without feeling selfish. Sometimes, it's as simple as self-compassion, remembering that we can't do everything, and that's OK. We do not have to save the world 24/7.

At other times, we may need to let others tend to us. Mr. Rogers, the American children's TV show host and Presbyterian minister, once said: "Taking care is one way to show your love. Another way is letting people take good care of you when you need it." This is hard for many of us strong, independent, giving types who don't want to seem needy. But the fact is that we need others, and sometimes we just can't do it alone. We were never meant to do it alone. Remember Collaboration?

This was brought home to me recently when I broke my wrist. I live in the countryside, and most of what I do all day involves physical labor—gardening, stacking wood, shoveling snow, or caring for animals. With my hand in a cast and sling, it was impossible to do many of my chores, let alone care for myself effectively. I had to let go of my self-sufficient pride and ask people to carry wood into the house to heat it, chop food so I could eat, and even wash and braid my hair since it was difficult to do with one hand.

It was profoundly humbling. I learned that I could not do everything, and as a consequence, I learned how much joy it gave people to help me and how grateful I was for their help. Even after my wrist healed, I made a point of gratefully accepting help when it was offered (and even asking for it!) instead of pretending I didn't need or want it.

We must re-imagine the phrase self-care to mean "care of the self," in line with what Thomas Moore called "care of the soul." In his book of the same name, Moore says, "Soul is not a thing but a quality or dimension of experiencing life and ourselves. It involves depth, value, relatedness, heart, and personal substance." In other words, everything we have been cultivating through the Ten Words thus far. To care for the depth and whole of ourselves, we must care for our souls.

We need to ask ourselves, "What do I need to thrive?" What does my soul or truest self need? That's the real definition of self-care. As the Dhammapada states, "If one knew oneself to be precious, One would guard oneself with care." If we don't practice self-care this way, we absolutely cannot be there to care for others.

CARE FOR THE WORLD

The Daode Jing verse 13 states, "Love the world as your own self; Then you can truly care for all things." If we are truly caring and loving for ourselves, we will recognize a tender place inside, aching not just for our own suffering but for the suffering of the world, whether people, plants and animals, or the planet. We will recognize a desire to relieve that suffering.

As we journey through Ten Words, our spiritual growth will quite naturally urge us to act in a way that expresses Care to relieve suffering. These days, it feels especially urgent. Many of us feel called to do something to change things and make them better or, as I say, "To leave the campground in better condition than you found it."

There are as many ways to care for the world as there are people.

True Care arises from the inside. It could be that your way of caring for the world is to care for your family and friends, or it could be in the form of stewarding the earth, caring for animals, making art, end-of-life work, social justice, or other public social action. It could be feeding people with homemade, healthy food, tending your garden, or reading bedtime stories to your kids. Every single thought, word, and action changes the world.

Civil Rights and children's activist Marian Wright Edelman said, "You really can change the world if you care enough." How you bring your practice of Care "off the cushion" is up to you. There are no rules, but it must come from your own exploration, practice, and calling. It must come from the things you care enough about to serve.

MEANING AND PURPOSE

There is a Japanese word, *ikigai*, which roughly translates to "purpose." It's why you wake up in the morning, what you care about, and your unique contribution to the world. What is your *ikigai*? What gets you up in the morning? What excites you? What do you love enough to give time to? What do you care about? What do you value? What makes your heart sing? And in what way will your contribution help the world thrive?

In Costa Rica, the same idea is known as *Plan de Vida* and means a sense of meaning in life. For many, meaning comes from caring for their land, animals, families, and communities. For some, it's their work as doctors, farmers, or teachers. For others, it's simply how they approach everything and everyone: with attention and the desire to do right by others. Care becomes the purpose and meaning of life, and caring for the world in whatever way we do helps us feel more connected, alive, and joyful.

Often, students asked my teacher, Lao Zhi Chang, "What are we supposed to do in the world?" Lao always laughed before responding, "Just do what is in front of you." We don't have to go halfway around the globe looking for ways to care for the world. There are endless opportunities to express care always right in front of your eyes. Just do what you can with what is in front of you in the way only you can. Care-fully.

I would propose that doing what gives you a sense of purpose and meaning and what shows up in front of you with care—even if it's just the dishes—is caring for the world. You don't have to lead a revolution or save the ocean; even the smallest act of care affects the world. As Indigenous rights activist Jessica Vega Ortéga says, "Maybe we can't change the world, but we can change the little piece that touches us."

Every "little piece that touches us" has a cumulative effect. Everyone's contribution adds up. If everyone just did what was in front of them to do—the little piece that touches them—from a place of service and Care, that might bring about what a rabbi friend of mine calls "The Messianic Era" or what some call "The Kingdom of God." At the very least, the world would be a nicer place to live. For all of us. Isn't that ultimately the point?

Why are we here? What's this all about? Simple: to love and serve your world. Anything less, you're wasting your time.

LAO ZHI CHANG, DAOIST ABBOT

REFLECTION QUESTIONS

1. What does Care mean to me?

2. Why is Care important to me?

3. In what ways do I express Care?

4. What do I love enough to care for?

5. What suffering moves me?

6. How do I practice self-care? Do I allow others to care for me?

7. How do I show care to others?

8. What is my *ikigai or Plan de Vida*? My sense of purpose or meaning?

9. How do I care for the world around me?

10. What is right in front of me, right now, that needs my care?

SUGGESTED PRACTICES

1. Make a list of what you care about. Resolve to show care for those people and things.

2. For one day, try to show care, in even the smallest way, to everyone and everything you encounter, no matter who or what.

3. In any relationship or situation, before you act, ask others, "What do you need?"

4. For one day, practice deep self-care. Ask yourself, "What do I need to thrive right now?"

5. For one day, notice everything in front of you that needs your care.

6. Choose something that matters to you and take one action—just one—to care for it.

PART 2

TEN WORDS FOR LIFE

The most important aspect of being on the spiritual path may be just to keep moving.

PEMA CHÖDRÖN

In Your Own Words

You have to be your own teacher and your own
disciple, and there is no teacher outside, no saviour, no
master; you yourself have to change, and therefore
you have to learn to observe, to know yourself.

J. KRISHNAMURTI

Now that you have explored each of the Ten Words, it's time to put your understanding into your own words. You can create your own unique set of personal guidelines, commitments, oaths, or vows for how you want to bring these practices into your life and into the service of building a better world. Like the vows taken by monastics, these guidelines will become your touchstone, compass, and personal path. How does what you have discovered help you become a better person, and how do you want to work towards making a better world?

We like to think of this as the "D" section of Ten Words. Discernment, Discipline, Dedication, and Devotion are all words and concepts that apply here and are common to all traditions. Without these attributes and the intention, or will, behind them, progress on any spiritual path is hindered. In monastic traditions, these attitudes are the fountain from which all activity springs. They are both the prerequisites and the results of following a spiritual path. The same is true for us if we want to become better people in a better world.

Through Discernment—the deep knowing that comes from an honest assessment of what is true or right for you—we find our authentic path. Living that path takes Discipline and Dedication. It's not easy to live a spiritually centered life; the world will challenge and test you. It takes Dedication to stick with it and Discipline to keep going through hard times. Lastly, Devotion is a step beyond Dedication: it is an unconditional love for the path you have chosen for yourself. Through Devotion to becoming better people in a better world, we put our practices first. It is through Devotion that we truly live from our spiritual center.

DISCERNMENT

Discernment is the process of assessing what is true, right, or useful for you in any situation. When it comes to writing your own commitments, it is in discerning contemplation, when we listen and attend to the voice of the Inner Teacher, the True Self, or the Divine, that we determine which values, beliefs, and behaviors we take to be true for us and decide to carry forward.

The process of Discernment takes time. Take one to two months to reflect and refine, listening for what you truly believe and want to embody. Don't rush the process; it's as much of an exploration as Ten Words itself. In many monastic traditions, this kind of process can take a year or more. Obviously, it doesn't have to take that long for you, but the point is to truly take the time to reflect on your spiritual path moving forward. If you can, take a short personal retreat, a weekend, or even a full day to focus on this. What do you truly understand and believe, and what commitments to yourself are you willing to make?

Hopefully, you kept notes on your journey because you will use them in the process of Discernment. What did you learn about yourself, others, and the world? What was most meaningful for you? What practices worked for you? What changed how you related to yourself, others, and the world around you? What did you discover about the Divine? What do you value, believe, and understand *as of this moment*? What will you do to become a better person in a better world?

DISCIPLINE

In all traditions, there are rules, guidelines, or teachings about how to behave every day that adherents try to follow. Whether we are talking about precepts or commandments, instructions, laws, or Rules of Life, they require a degree of Discipline to enact. They aren't designed to be easy; they are aspirations that take effort. After all, you don't get good at anything without some degree of effort and discipline. Just ask any pianist.

In many traditions, this Discipline takes the form of vows or commitments, statements that describe the actions a follower will take on a moment-to-moment basis moving forward. These vows are aspirations, too. They require Discipline to uphold. At this point in the process, you are invited to write your own Vows.

Your Vows will be no different than any other vows; you must consider them your personal set of commitments that you will try your absolute best to be disciplined about keeping. But consider this: vows are just extended practices. They aren't "perfects." You are not committing to be perfect, just to keep trying.

If you don't like the idea of taking a "vow," you can call them your Precepts (like Buddhists and Daoists), your Yoga (like Hindus), your *Mitzvot* (like Jews), your Pillars (after Islam), or your Rule of Life (after the Benedictines), or just your Promises. You could also just call them your Practices (which is what they are). The important part is that these attitudes and actions will guide every thought, word, and deed of your life every day, and you will be disciplined and dedicated to them.

Writing Your Vows

To write your Vows or Commitments, go back through your journal and look carefully at what you wrote about each of the Ten Words. Note anything that stood out to you that gives you an action point. This is important. We are not looking for beliefs but how we put those beliefs into practice. Look at how specific practices changed you. Notice what happened because of something you did. For example, if you found you had less anxiety when you spent a few minutes each day in meditation, note that. If you discovered that your relationships improved when you put your needs aside and looked for the win/win, make a note.

Though your Vows could simply be the Ten Words themselves, make them personal. Ideally, let your Vows be based on the Ten Words but more specific. For example, if I look at Attention, I notice that when I pay wholehearted attention to what is happening in the present moment, I find myself happier, calmer, and more engaged. When I spend a few moments each day in quiet attention, I notice that the rest of my day is more attentive. If I reflect on Collaboration, I find that when I replace "Me" with "We," my relationships improve, and I am more concerned with the well-being of others. I notice that when

I give others' needs equal weight with my own, there is less conflict and more productivity.

The important thing here is to look for the specifics of how each of the Ten Words was expressed for you. Ask yourself:

- What did you experience that made the word come to life?
- What did you change?
- What practices helped?
- What words were most meaningful?
- What worked for you?
- What do you not want to forget?

From these notes, write simple statements that you can commit to practicing and enacting. These statements are the *how* of becoming a better person in a better world. For example, "I commit to taking a few moments each day to be present to the present moment" or "I commit to putting others' needs on equal footing with my own." Notice that these statements aren't plain restatements of the Ten Words but elaborations or expansions based on how you experienced them. They should be specific, but the simpler they are, the better.

Don't commit yourself to generalities that give you too much leeway or to things that are beyond your capacity or so idealistic that you are doomed to fail from the beginning. Don't over-commit yourself, either. Stick with what you truly believe you can and want to do, even if it requires stretching. Remember, these are practices, not perfects. We will always forget and often fall short of our most well-meaning aspirations; we will always stray from the path. But, if we can recall the simple commitments that we have made for ourselves, we can come back more easily.

Try to write at least one Vow or Commitment for each of the Ten Words. You may find that you want to write several for each word and then distill them into one or two. If you need to write a paragraph, do so. There is no right way to do this; just be as honest as you can be with yourself. You don't get points for aspiring to sainthood or false humility. Allow your commitments to be something you reach for, not something you do without thinking. Stretch yourself.

Your final list should be between five to ten statements, Vows, or Commitments. Too many, and you will be overwhelmed. Too few and you might be cutting yourself short. The point is that your commitments should be easy for you to remember and represent concrete action points that you think are within your reach (even if it's a *big* stretch). They should describe ways of being and behaving that help you bring your beliefs and understandings to reality every moment of every day. Here are a few examples:

- "I commit to giving everyone and everything I encounter the gift of my fullest attention."

- "I vow to treat all of life with kindness, remembering that I would want the same for myself."

- "I strive for harmony by allowing myself and others to follow their path without interference."

- "I promise to treat all beings as my brothers and sisters, whose value is equal to my own."

- "I will take time each day for my meditation practice."

- "I choose to give generously of my time in the service of others for a minimum of five hours each month."

Remember, these Vows or Commitments are your personal discipline based on what you know and have experienced up until now. Note that these may change, evolve, or become even more specific over time, but for now, this is the path you commit to walking and the steps you will take along that path.

DEDICATION

Once you have written your Commitments or Vows, it is time to dedicate yourself to upholding them. This is done through a ceremony or ritual where you speak your Vows aloud and promise to keep them. Not unlike a wedding ceremony or ordination, you will publicly (even if it's just to your dog, a tree, or the Divine) state your dedication to the Vows you have written and do your best to keep them.

Dedication doesn't end with the ceremony, however. Dedication, like Discipline, is daily. We must constantly remind ourselves that these are the Vows we have taken and that we are dedicated to upholding them, even—and especially—when it is hard. Taking our Vows is only half the story; the bigger part is how we dedicate ourselves to practicing what we preach.

Taking Your Vows

As we noted in Celebration, ritual can be powerful. The right ritual, held with respect and reverence, can fundamentally alter our way of seeing and being in the world. Ritual taps into the subconscious and transforms us.

For your own ritual of Vow Taking (or, as I like to think of it, Vow Offering or Vow Accepting), you might choose to be alone in nature or gather with friends or family. The important part is that you must speak your Vows aloud, whether someone is there to hear them or not. Even if there is no other person there, there are beings, and there is the Divine. Speaking your Vows aloud makes them real, not just ideas on paper. In all traditions, the spoken word is powerful.

Before, during, or after you state your Vows, you might choose to light a candle, plant a tree, change a piece of clothing, bow, or do some other physical action that is symbolic of your commitment. One person tattooed a few meaningful words on his arm before the ritual. Another placed a statue of Guan Yin, the Chinese Goddess of Compassion, in a special garden she created as her meditation spot during the ritual. In my community, we tie a string bracelet of 10 strands around our left wrist that we wear each day. Find a symbolic act that works for you. Again, there is no right way to do this. But take your time in designing the ritual that will be most meaningful for you.

Living Your Vows

Once you have committed to your Vows, put them somewhere where you will see them every day. We are forgetful beings and need reminders. This is part of remaining dedicated to your vows: remembering. You can write your Vows in the front of your journal or on a piece of paper that you hang in a place you see daily. You can record them and play them back before sitting for meditation or while you are walking. You can even put them on sticky notes and place them all over your home—anything you can do to keep them in front of you on a regular basis.

My Vows are written in ink calligraphy on a scroll that hangs behind my altar. Each day, when I sit to meditate, I read through them before settling into silence. Others put them in their journals to use as a kind of *Lectio Divina*, choosing one statement each day to contemplate. One student made her Vows into a poem she repeats to herself many times a day.

However, just reading or reciting your Vows isn't the whole of it. You must practice and do what you said you would do. That means you might want to keep a daily or weekly accounting of what works and what doesn't, a kind of spiritual ledger. This is a technique used in some monastic traditions to train novices to practice their vows. It might feel rigid at first, but it's simply a means to an end. Keeping "score" helps you track whether you are keeping your Vows and your actions at the forefront of your mind, and how well it's working for you.

To do this, list your Vows on a piece of paper, and each evening or once a week, go through them and write down what you did—or didn't do—to uphold that Vow. You can also use your Vow review as part of a journaling practice. Don't use this as a reward/punishment device, but rather as a way of bringing awareness to your practice of Vows, or where you are in terms of walking your talk.

Remember, sometimes we hit the mark, and other times, we fall short. That's OK. No one is asking for perfection, just a good, solid attempt to do your best in each moment and the awareness of when you could have done better. In Hebrew, the word is *Teshuvah*, or repentance, and it is how we return to our center. We literally "turn around." We just keep coming back to what we know.

Through the dedicated practice of your Vows, your commitment to becoming a better person in a better world strengthens. At some point, you might find that the Vows you have taken become automatic; you don't have to think about being kind or doing your meditation practice. You don't have to keep track anymore (though it's good to check in with yourself every so often). It just becomes who you are and the way you act in the world. Basically, the more you do it, the easier it gets, and without even noticing, you are living and acting from your spiritual center most of the time.

DEVOTION

Like Dedication, Devotion is how we live fully from our spiritual center. To be devoted to someone or something is to put that being or thing first above all others: to be faithful, loyal, or loving. If we are devoted to something, it is because we truly love it.

We must remember that just writing or taking our Vows and being dedicated to upholding them is only part of the process; we must be in love with our spiritual journey. We must be steadfast in our desire to continually explore, grow, and expand our understanding of how to become a better person in a better world. We must love our path to truly live it. That takes Devotion.

Loving Your Life and Path

Your devotion to your Vows and becoming a better person in a better world means that everything you do is because you love and are faithful to your understanding, values, and beliefs. Your Vows — and the continual inquiry of them — are the center of your being. They are the foundation for your life. Loving your life means loving your spiritual path, too. You don't give up just because something more attractive or convenient comes along. You hold fast to it like one in a storm would hold fast to a lifeline.

That doesn't mean Vows won't change. Your Vows are a living document. Humans, like landscapes, change over time. Your Vows, while an accurate description of your current state of understanding and commitment to becoming a better person in a better world, will change as you do. However, you will only be able to notice the changes and adapt to them if you are consistently practicing your Vows and Ten Words. As Zhuangzi, the 6th Century BCE Daoist Sage, said, "The path is made by walking on it."

You can—and should—go back through the Ten Words regularly as you continue your journey, paying attention to new insights you have. You can go back through in order or just choose one at a time to explore again. The Ten Words have tremendous depth; your experiences as you continue to explore each word will reveal many layers of understanding and meaning. Each time you revisit them, your experience will be different. In addition to your own new experiences, you might find readings in wisdom teachings that offer new ways of seeing or embodying the Ten Words.

It's a good idea to review your Vows annually, noting where you could be more specific, or, if need be, where you could loosen up. You can reassess your intention and restate our commitment to your Vows. Every time you return to your Vows and the Ten Words, your commitment to becoming a better person in a better world deepens. Just like a loving relationship, the stronger your commitment, the stronger the love can grow. This is a journey for a lifetime. The longer you walk, the more interesting it gets.

> *What if our religion was each other? If our practice*
> *was our life? What if the temple was the Earth? If*
> *forests were our church? If holy water — the rivers,*
> *lakes, and oceans? What if meditation was our*
> *relationships? If the Teacher was life? If wisdom was*
> *knowledge? If love was the center of our being?*
>
> **GANGA WHITE**

REFLECTION QUESTIONS

1. What did I learn about myself, others, and the world?

2. What was most meaningful for me?

3. Which words or phrases stood out for me?

4. What practices worked for me?

5. What changed how I related to myself, others, and the world around me?

6. What did I discover about the Divine?

7. What do I value, believe, and understand *as of this moment*?

8. What are my highest spiritual aspirations?

9. What can I do each day to support my spiritual practice?

10. To what will I devote myself?

11. How can I be more disciplined about my spiritual practice?

12. What does becoming a better person in a better world look like for me?

SUGGESTED PRACTICES

1. For each of the Ten Words, write five to ten words or phrases that exemplify your understanding of that word and the specific actions that you could take to make that understanding a practice.

2. Refine those words or phrases into five to ten separate vows you are willing to take.

3. Think about rituals or practices you can do each day, week, or month to support your spiritual life. What are they?

4. Think about what types of celebrations would support your spiritual life. List them.

5. Design a small ritual in which you speak your vows aloud. Make sure to include a physical, symbolic act to help you remember that moment.

6. Write your vows and place them somewhere you will see them regularly.

7. Commit to practicing your vows.

8. Keep a journal about how you bring your vows into practice. What works and what doesn't?

9. Keep learning, growing, practicing, and reviewing Ten Words and your vows.

10. Enjoy the journey!

A Better World,
Word-by-Word

*The work is plentiful... It is not your duty to finish
the work, but neither are you at liberty to neglect it.*

PIRKEI AVOT 2:15-16

Now that you have explored each of the Ten Words and
written Vows, the question emerges: How do I bring my
spiritual life authentically into the world? In these changing and challenging times, how can I be of service? How can I help
build a better world?

One of the tenets of interspirituality is to take our spiritual practice
off the mat and to embed and embody it in our lives and the world
around us. We cannot just keep all our hard work to ourselves. Service is an extension or amplification of Care. The world needs people who care—and act on that care. Now, more than ever.

If you are practicing the Ten Words, you will discover that each
word has the potential to change the world. From Attention to Care,
the capacities we cultivate translate into action, and at some point,

you will naturally feel an urge to do something that might make the world a better place.

For each of us, that "something" will be different. Not all of us are activists, nor do we have to be. For many of us, our "action" in the world is simply caring for our friends and families, being kind to others, and serving when and where we can. That is enough.

For others, that urge to serve may be bigger. We might feel called to work for justice, protest, make art, write, or speak out. Everything we do from an authentic place of care and service counts. Everything. As the quote above states, we don't have to save the world (we can't), but what matters is that we do *something*. We do what we can. Word-by-word, minute-by-minute.

WHAT IS SERVICE?

Contemporary spiritual teacher Andrew Harvey calls on us to pursue what he calls "Sacred Activism." For him, that means doing what you can to help make the world a better place and aid the evolution of consciousness toward compassion and love. Activism, however, is a loaded term for some, implying that we must all be out in the streets with placards and bullhorns, shouting and fighting for social or political change. Sometimes, that level of action is needed, but not every act of service requires forceful change. In fact, many don't, and most shouldn't.

For that reason, we prefer the more inclusive, less aggressive term, Sacred Service. Sacred Service means that our actions in the world come from our innermost being and stem from a deep reverence for—and attunement to—the Sacred, or whatever we understand as bigger than ourselves. Service can be small or large—just changing our mind is a service that can change the world! But no matter what we do, our actions must arise from an authentic desire to serve, not to fix, not from external pressure, and certainly not from our egos.

If we serve because we feel we must or to fulfill our ego needs, our service will be less effective, and we will not derive joy from it. Instead, we will get stuck in pride or resentment. If we serve out of fear, our service risks causing more harm than good. However, if we listen for what is honestly calling to us from our truest selves through our contemplative practice, we will act in the world from a sacred, attentive, and care-full place, and our service will enrich us all.

FINDING YOUR CALLING

We each must find our own way of serving the world. Quaker writer, teacher, and activist Parker J. Palmer says, "Our deepest calling is to grow into our own authentic self-hood, whether or not it conforms to some image of who we ought to be. As we do so, we will not only find the joy that every human being seeks—we will also find our path of authentic service in the world."

Likewise, in the Bible, it is noted that "We have different gifts, according to the grace given to each of us. If it is to encourage, then give encouragement; if it is giving, then give generously; if it is to lead, do it diligently; if it is to show mercy, do it cheerfully" (Romans 12:6-8). Knowing ourselves authentically, what we love, and what we can offer that the world needs is the key to authentic, joyful service. We must use our contemplative practice to truly listen to what arises in us. What calls to you from your deepest self?

In his book, *Let Your Heartbreak Be Your Guide*, New Monastic leader and Episcopal priest Adam Bucko suggests that you follow your heartbreak. What breaks your heart enough to want to do something about it? For many of us, that can be an overwhelming question. There is so much suffering in the world; where do we start?

One way of thinking about it is to ask what is intolerable to you personally. What makes your personal world unbearable? Is it the suffering of animals? Of the planet? Or is it hunger? Injustice? War? Is it the suffering of your own family or friends? Father Bucko suggests that you allow yourself to feel the pain of those heartbreaks and, from a contemplative place, explore what it is that you can and want to do to relieve the suffering of another.

For some, that heartbreak might be so painful that it turns into anger. While outrage can be useful in getting your attention, it's not a good place from which to serve. Outrage can blind you to what is really happening. It can lead to reactive and rash actions that contribute to ongoing suffering or, at worst, are deeply destructive. However, directed through contemplative practice and the Ten Words, outrage can lead you to what matters enough to you to act in an appropriate way that serves the greater good with care.

There is another way of approaching it, as we discussed in Care. If we only truly care for the things we love, what do you love enough to care for? What do you love enough not to lose? To preserve? To support or to enrich? If we come to our service in the world from the place of love, we will want the object of our love to thrive, so we will do what we can to support that. Love will naturally act with kindness, generosity, and compassion as long as we remember that the most loving action we can take is to support others in getting their needs met, not imposing our own beliefs and desires on them in the name of "love."

Whether we come from heartbreak or love, we must be mindful of reducing people and situations to problems we must solve, fix, or change. Everyone and everything has layers of depth and whole-ness. When we reduce them to just "a problem," we diminish them, which can be more hurtful. We miss the fullness of their being or their complexity. We also risk serving from a sense of superiority or intellectualism, thinking we know what is needed to fix whatever we see as the problem. That reduces us, as well. We must see and serve from our wholeness: our heads, hearts, and hands.

Ultimately, our calling to service, which comes from deep within ourselves and our connection to the Divine, will be part of what helps us feel alive, engaged, and connected. Jack Kornfield reminds us, "What is truly a part of our spiritual path is that which brings us alive. If gardening brings us alive, that is part of our path; if it is music, if it is conversation…we must follow what brings us alive."

BEING AS DOING

Our doing should be an extension of our very being. But for some, *being* is *doing*. I will never forget being in the presence of a Buddhist nun in the Himalayas, whose mere being radiated such love that every-one and everything in her orbit felt cared for, accepted, and whole. She did nothing, but nothing was left undone. For weeks after meet-ing her, I felt like I was walking on air, and she became an inspira-tion for me. How could I, simply by *being*, care for the world with such love and ease? Who would I have to become?

I have been fortunate to meet many other people in my life who exuded a similar kind of effortless love. I've met nurses in hospitals, teachers in schools, and even people at the checkout counter of the grocery store whose very being was transformative. None of these people were doing anything special. They weren't trying to save the world. Most of them were just doing their jobs, but they did them with humility, care, and love—and something of their being shone through. They were "helpful beings," not "being helpful."

You do not have to be an enlightened master to be a loving presence for others. Simply by cultivating the qualities and behaviors we have been practicing through Ten Words, every interaction you have with another being can change the world. Sometimes, the best thing we can do is just listen. Bear witness. Just be present to whatever someone else is going through without doing anything.

"Be love" is the phrase that floats around. Philosopher Simone Weil once defined love as "To feel with one's whole self the existence of another being." We all have the capacity to feel the wholeness of another's existence from our own wholeness and to become a more loving presence for others. From that place, our service will naturally arise.

A VESSEL

Christian mystic Hildegard of Bingen said, "A human being is a vessel that God has built for himself and filled with his inspiration so that his works are perfected in it." If we can remember that it's never "us" doing anything, but we are only vessels for the doing, there is deep humility in service. The recognition takes us out of our pride or sense of accomplishment, as well as our fear of failure or inadequacy.

Likewise, Teresa of Avila was famous for saying that Christ had no hands in the world, so we must be his hands in service. In other words, we could say that we are the Divine *doing*, or the Divine is *doing* through us. There is a beautiful surrender in this idea. It's not really you doing it; it is simply being done through you. It can be done through anyone and everyone.

In their book, *How Can I Help?* Ram Dass and Paul Gorman speak about how our sense of separateness from others affects our ability to serve. It creates barriers of identity: helper and helped. If we remember that separateness is an illusion, that we are not separate from the Divine and are all interconnected, then those we serve are no less vessels for the Divine than we are. We meet there on level ground. Who is serving whom? Who is being served? Perhaps both and neither. It's another way to put our sense of service into perspective.

RESISTANCE TO SERVICE

The desire to serve is natural to us. We do it all the time, whether we are conscious of it or not. But sometimes, we resist service, feeling as if we have nothing to give or that giving will be too difficult or somehow beneath us. We all have something to offer one another: a hand, an ear, a shoulder, a smile, a hug, a word. None of those things take special skills or much effort.

We must be careful not to let the weight of the world or the depth of someone's pain overwhelm us. We don't want to get trapped in our own self-image of insufficiency or grandeur. Remember, we can only do what we can. And if we just can't do anything—or as much as we would like to—right now, that's OK, too. We do not have to be the savior.

There is a season for service, and, like everything else, times and people change. What called to you last year may be different than this year. What might have been useful last week is no longer needed this week. Today, you may be caring for your family; tomorrow, planting trees. Today, you may feel the urge to write or speak out on an issue; tomorrow, you might feel called to help a neighbor rake leaves. Today, you might just need to take time off; tomorrow, you will be ready to serve.

The urge to serve takes many different forms at different times. What is yours to do *right now?* And right *now* is the point. As we return to the first of the Ten Words, Attention, we are called to be present to the present moment. What calls to you *now?* What is alive for you *now?* What does the world need *now?* What can you do *now?* Who can you be *now?*

Remember that we are not in control of the world. We are not in control of other people. We are not in control of what happens next at any moment. All we can ever do is be present to what is happening now, respond appropriately, and do the best we can from a place of humility and love. We do what we can to "Leave the campground in better condition than we found it" today, even if it's just to sit in awe of what is before us. Then, maybe tomorrow we will find ourselves living in a better world.

Where do we begin? Begin with the heart.

JULIAN OF NORWICH

REFLECTION QUESTIONS

1. What calls to me from my deepest self?

2. What is mine to do?

3. What do I care about?

4. What resistance do I have to service?

5. What breaks my heart enough to want to do something about it?

6. What do I love enough to care for?

7. What do I love enough about not to lose? To preserve? To support or to enrich?

8. What skills or talents do I have that the world needs right now?

9. What could I learn that would be useful?

10. Who do I have to become to be a loving presence for someone?

11. What is right in front of me?

12. What is reaching out for my heart and hand?

13. What would give me joy to give?

14. How can I be a loving, serving presence in the world?

15. What can I do, and who can I be right *now*?

SUGGESTED PRACTICES

1. Pay attention to all the little ways you serve every day. Write them down.

2. Call a friend you haven't spoken to in a long time and ask, "How are you?" Then listen. Just listen.

3. Join your local mutual aid society or other volunteer group and offer a few hours a month. Pay attention to how volunteering makes you feel.

4. Go to a park or natural area and pick up any trash you find.

5. Choose one thing that calls to you and do one thing, just one *now*, that serves that.

Conclusion

Not all who wander are lost.
J.R.R. TOLKIEN

I t's strange to call this a conclusion because, in truth, there is no conclusion to a spiritual journey, and there's no final word on life. If there is, I certainly don't have it. None of us ever really knows where our life or spiritual path will lead us. They are, after all, the same thing, and both are unpredictable. There are lots of twists and turns. There are no right ways or answers, and there are no guarantees. There's no test at the end. The best we can do to become better people in a better world is to take to heart the saying of one of my dearest teachers, Daoist Abbot Lao Zhi Chang: "Follow the Way, and that's enough."

Ten Words is not *the* way, and it's not the *only* way, but it is *a* way, something to guide you to becoming the better person you want to be in a world that supports all. It might take you into new, undiscovered territory, but at least you will have a map to give you some sense of direction. Ten Words has given many people greater joy, ease, purpose, and a new way of becoming better people in a better world. For some, it has utterly transformed their lives.

I can't promise you it will be easy. Anyone who does is lying. In fact, I can assure you that you will have many moments of wanting to give up, go home, put your feet up, and turn on the TV. That's OK. It happens. No one says you must be perfect. Go easy on yourself. Remember that you don't have to get anywhere but where you are at any moment. Even though we talk about becoming better people, we are always in that process. Just be where you are and who you are. Go step-by-step. Pause and enjoy the view. There's no rush. Take your time.

§

As I continue to practice the Ten Words, I find that my understanding of what it means to become a better person in a better world is a process of perpetual inquiry. But the journey has led me to a few conclusions thus far. I can sum it up in a single sentence: if the Divine-Of-My-Understanding is none other than Life itself, then being a better person in a better world means doing everything in my power to support Life—mine, others, the myriad creatures and plants and other beings that share this beautiful, crazy world with me—and to do so with joy, reverence, and love.

That means I am always working through the Ten Words—Attention, Acceptance, Authenticity, Benevolence, Balance, Contemplation, Creativity, Collaboration, Celebration, and Care—and the vows I wrote related to them. It means that anything I say or do *must* be filtered through those understandings and commitments. Am I walking my talk?

I will be the first to admit that I don't always do it. There are times that I forget or am too tired, stressed, or worried. I get confused. I slip up. I am human, after all, and if we've learned anything from our thousands of years of trying to be decent, kind people in a world that supports life, it's not easy. But we keep trying. That's why we need guidance and support. That's why we have maps for the journey to get us back on track.

I don't have it right yet, and I may never, but along the way, I picked up a few tips I can share that might make your own journey more productive and enjoyable.

- Don't weigh yourself down with things you don't need, like old ideas, assumptions, beliefs, or fears.

- Go easy on yourself. There's no rush and there's no perfection. Self-compassion is needed.

- Remember to take care of your Foundations: eat, drink, sleep, rest, relax, play, and connect with others.

- Keep an open mind, a willing heart, and a sense of humor.

- Let go of outcomes. You aren't in control. Just do what you can now, in each moment.

- Build a spiritual community or a few good friends to share the joys and challenges.

- And most of all, have a good map.

If you stay on your path, even in the hard times, you will learn a great deal about yourself, others, the world, whatever you experience as Sacred, and this amazing, beautiful, improbable, messy thing we call Life. You will find yourself becoming kinder, happier, healthier, more peaceful and fulfilled, and navigating the ups and downs of our changing world with more purpose, joy and connection. As you change for the better, the world changes. And if more people do it, we might all find ourselves living in a better world.

Made in the USA
Middletown, DE
03 September 2024